I0608878

İlhan Berk

ALSO BY İLHAN BERK, IN GEORGE MESSO'S TRANSLATION

A Leaf About to Fall. Selected Poems †
Madrigals *
Letters & Sound
The Book of Things *

* published by Shearsman Books
† out of print

İlhan Berk

New Selected Poems 1947–2008

translated from Turkish by

George Messo

Shearsman Books

First published in the United Kingdom in 2016 by
Shearsman Books
50 Westons Hill Drive
Emersons Green
BRISTOL
BS16 7DF

Shearsman Books Ltd Registered Office
30–31 St. James Place, Mangotsfield, Bristol BS16 9JB
(this address not for correspondence)

www.shearsman.com

ISBN 978-1-84861-461-1

Copyright © İlhan Berk, 2006, 2008
Copyright © the Estate of İlhan Berk, 2009, 2014, 2016

Translations © George Messo, 2006, 2008, 2009, 2014, 2016

The right of George Messo to be identified as the translator
of this work has been asserted by him in accordance with the
Copyrights, Designs and Patents Act of 1988.
All rights reserved.

ACKNOWLEDGEMENTS
The poems included here are extracted from four previously published books:
A Leaf About To Fall: Selected Poems (Salt Publishing, 2006),
Madrigals (Shearsman Books, 2008), *The Book of Things* (Salt Publishing, 2009;
2nd edition, Shearsman Books, 2016), and *Letters & Sounds* (RHB, 2014).

Many of the translations first appeared in
*Absinthe, Dialogue of Nations through Poetry in Translation, Bülent,
Near East Review, Orient Express, Other Poetry, Shadow Train, Shearsman,
The American Reader, The Argotist* and *Turkish Book Review*.

The translator wishes to express his gratitude to
The Baltic Centre for Writers and Translators in Gotland, Sweden,
where these translations began.

Contents

Preface   10
Context and Counter-Current:
    Introducing İlhan Berk   11

1947-1975

Tree   16
Kızılırmak   17
A Forest in the South   18
The Grieving Stream   19
The Flower's Indescribable Grief: Yellow Crocus   20
Saint-Antoine's Pigeons
    I.   Eleni's Hands   21
    II.   Youth   21
    III. Saint-Antoine's Time of Lovemaking   24
    IV. Childhood in Fener   25
    V.   Morning   26
    VI. Eleni Light   27
    VII. Sky   28
Arma Virumque Cano
    I.   Saturday Darkness   29
    II.   Ramparts   29
    III. Little   30
    IV. Map of the Firmament   31
    V.   The Gate of Ahmet I   31
    VI. Invitation   31
Water Days I, II, III, IV, V, VI   32
Season of the Hunt
    Prologue   34
    I.   The Hunt   35
    II.   The Women   36
    III. The Rampart   37
    IV. The Child   38
    V.   The Men   39
    VI. Upstairs…   40
    VII. Flow   41
    VIII. Me   42

IX. Sefine   43
Epilogue   44

You   45
Istanbul   46
from Woodcuts
   Steppe   52
   Yeşilyurt Street   52
   Country Life   52
   Autumn   53
   Sun   53
   Sunset   53
   Picture   54
   Window   54
   Plane Tree Leaf   54

1978-1982

The Thames   56
A Street Leads Down to the Sea   65
Paris   67
Sofia   73
Forest   74
For Homer   75
The Sea Book
   I.   Chaws   76
   II. Threewells Street   76
   III. The City   77
   IV. Hay   77
   V.   Those from Karya   78
   VI. Ecology   78
Reading Li Po   79
Novembers   80
The History of a Face
   I.   History   81
   II. Voice   81
   III. Exile   82
Inscription on a Grave   83

Dead

    I. On the Frontier of Pain   84
    II. Death   84
    III. About to Leave   85
    IV. Death was Scrutinized   85
An Old Street in Pera   86
Poem for a Father Looking for his Lost Son   87
What a Woman Sees Each Night from a Coast   88
An Old Salt   89
View   90
The Man Walking along a Sunny Coast   91
Visiting the Beloved Wife of a Dead Poet   92
Old Boatmen   93
Evening with a Sprig of Basil   94
The Men   94
As if Death were a Daily Routine   95
A Shoreside Coffeehouse   96
Book of the Dead
    On the Painful Death of a Discoverer   98
    Conversations on the Life of an Exalted Person,
        According to Ibn-i Hacer Heytemi   99
I Woke Saying I love You Three Times   100
Poet and Voices   101
Hamam Street   102
The Women   103
In the Sea's Wake   104
from The Secret History of Poetry   105

1984-1996

from Delta and Child
    Passer-by   110
    Sage   110
    Clocks   110
    Quince   110
    Autumn   111
    Birds   111
    Forest   111
    Tobacco   111

Black Amber   112
Now As a Little Rose Goes Through the World   113
Each Day I Walk From One End of a Market to the Other   114
Thank You   115
Beautiful River   116
Yesterday I Wasn't at Home, I Took to the Hills   117
There Have Been Trees I Have Made Friends With   118
Letters and Sounds   119
Whichever Angle We Take, Everything Explains Itself   120
I Don't Want to Think   121
Askelopis   122
Rocks   123
Towards Evening   124
Fern   124
Garden   124
Death is like Nothing Else   125
Leaf   125
Shadow falls across the Courtyard   125
Stopping   126
Goat Track   126
As I Write   127
Ashes and End   127
What the Tree Says   127
Trees   128
Words II   128
Blonde Haired Child   128

1997-2008

from THINGS THAT COUNT THINGS THAT DON'T
    Lyre   130
    Stones   133
    Golden Oriole   136
    Table   138
    Roundness   146
    Slug   149
    Bra   152
    Mud   154

Sparrow   157
Dot/Dash   159

from LONG LIVE NUMBERS   162

from HOUSE
   Door   179
   Room   181
   Window   182
   Wall   183

A Turtledove Valantin Taskin   189
Denizens of Hristaki Arcade   190
Nevizade Street Greengrocer Ahmet Aslanoğlu   194

MADRIGALS
   I Came to You Always with a Piece of Sky   195
   Small Villages Birds Cats Dogs   195
   It's True I Sometimes Turn to Rivers and Trees   196
   A River Moves Around Like a Peasant   196
   It Was Then the Self-Explaining World Came…   197
   That Was You Thin As a Leaf   197
   It Should Be Evening Where You Are Now   198
   We Used to Use a Water Clock & a Sundial   198
   As If We Were Like Blacked Out Days   199
   Ask Night About Me in Time and Space   199

Translator's Preface to this Edition

New Selected Poems updates, expands, and replaces my previous selection, *A Leaf About to Fall*, published in 2006. All of the poems published there are reprinted here, some with minor revisions, alongside substantial new selections from three subsequent books in English: *Madrigals* (2008), *The Book of Things* (2009; 2nd edition, 2016) and *Letters & Sound* (2014). For the present edition the poems are presented chronologically, stretching across the length of Berk's long writing life, from 1947 and the appearance of his first book, to 2008, the year in which he died, aged 90, at his home in Bodrum.

A decade ago Berk was virtually unknown outside of Turkey. Today his strange, beautiful, surprising poems have been heard in almost every corner of the English-speaking world. His audience, admittedly small, is one that grows, in breadth and in depth. I hope this new selection continues to carry his voice.

George Messo
2016

Context and Counter-Current
— Introducing İlhan Berk —

İlhan Berk was born in 1918 in the Aegean city of Manisa. He once said "If a poem is written and goes out into the world, something in the world has changed." Berk's poems have been changing the world of Turkish poetry for the best part of seven decades. His innovative poetics have marked him out as one of the vital modernising forces in contemporary Turkish literature and earned him a reputation as a literary *enfant terrible*, even an "extremist." Yet others deride his linguistic experimentalism as the work of a "French renegade." Few poets in Turkey today would dispute the significance of his work. Even in the year of his death, at the tender age of 90, more productive than ever, Berk remained a force to be reckoned with.

İlhan Berk graduated from Necatibey Teacher Training College in Balikesir and, after two years as a primary-school teacher in Espiye, Giresun, entered Gazi Institute of Education (now Gazi University) in Ankara, graduating from the department of French in 1944. From 1945 to 1955 he taught French at various secondary schools and colleges in Zonguldak, Samsun and Kırşehir. In 1956 he joined the publications department of the state-owned Ziraat Bank as a translator, where he stayed until his retirement in 1969.

His first poems appeared as early as the 1930's in magazines like *Varlık* (Presence) and *Uyanış* (Awakening). His first book, *Guneşi Yakanların Selamı* (Greetings of the Sun Burners, 1935), published by the Manisa Community Centre, was strongly influenced by the poetry of Nazım Hikmet. Yet even by the 1930s Turkish poetry was barely out of the Ottoman court, cramped by convention and seemingly marooned in a netherworld of post-symbolism. Hikmet, who had almost single-handedly set about upturning the status quo, was by 1938 serving a prison sentence for treason, his books banned. Much of Hikmet's revolutionary poetic credo, his belief that poetry should address the social and political concerns of everyday folk in a language free of artifice and intellectual pretention, lived on into the following decade in *Varlık*, a magazine to which Berk continued to contribute alongside leading "First New" poets Melih Cevdet Anday, Oktay Rifat and Orhan Veli Kanık. It was Kanık who nailed the *First New* movement's controversial manifesto in his collection, *Garip* (Strange, 1941):

The literary taste on which the new poetry will base itself is no longer the taste of a minority class... The question is not to make a defence of class interests, but merely to explore the people's tastes, to determine them, and to make them reign supreme over art... In order to rescue ourselves from the stifling effects of the literatures which have dictated and shaped our tastes and judgments for too many years, we must dump overboard everything that those literatures have taught us. We wish it were possible to dump even language itself...[1]

Berk's subsequent poems of this period, in *Istanbul* (1947), *Günaydın Yeryüzü* (*Good morning Earth*, 1952), *Türkiye Şarkısı* (*Song of Turkey*, 1953) and *Köroğlu* (1955, named after a sixteenth century folk hero and wandering minstrel) relied heavily on early modernist strategies of the *First New*. But Berk was seldom, if ever, ideologically driven. The ambitious scope of his early books, their oracular, legend-telling quality, the colloquial musical structures and rhythms prompted one critic to dub him "the Turkish Walt Whitman." In 1953, however, two years before the last and most accomplished of his "Whitman period" books, *Köroğlu*, Berk made a sudden and decisive break. The publication of his poem 'Saint-Antoine's Pigeons' in the magazine *Yenilik* was to signal a paradigm shift in Turkish poetry, as pervasive and fundamental as the *First New*, a movement which would later be known as the "Second New."

Both the *First New* and the *Second New* were responses to Turkey's volatile, reactionary social and political landscape. Just as the War of Independence had dramatically transformed Turkey from a Sultanate into a modern Republic, so too the *First New* had dragged Turkish poetry, somewhat belatedly, into the twentieth century. By the end of World War II, however, the reformist platform of the first Republican government was beginning to look hollow. The routine arrest and imprisonment of left-wing activists, writers and intellectuals defined the increasingly hostile and conservative political ethos. By the late 1940s the painfully slow rate of reforms led to Turkey's first multi-party election, amid widespread feelings of disillusionment and betrayal, feelings which many on the political left were now wary to voice for fear of arrest. It is little wonder, then, that the *First New*'s naive, optimistic celebrations

---

[1] Quoted in Halman, T.S. 'Introduction' in *Just For The Hell of It: 111 Poems by Orhan Veli Kanık*, Multilingual Foreign Language Press, Istanbul, 1997.

of everyday life seemed to many poets, including Berk, tragically out of place at a time when freedoms to speak on social issues were being so violently suppressed. With bitter irony it was the same incoming far-right nationalist government of Adnan Menderes which initiated Nazım Hikmet's release, following a general amnesty of political prisoners, a government which was to preside over one of the darkest and most politically repressive periods in the Republic's history. Indeed, it was Hikmet's fear of re-arrest that had him flee Turkey only six months after his release.

It was into such a climate that Berk's now famous poem 'Saint-Antoine's Pigeons' fell, with its fragmentation, its disruptive grammatical juxtapositions, its sexually suggestive and historically-minded rhetoric, its radical and shocking disavowal of the *First New*'s "public language". What began with 'Saint-Antoine's Pigeon's' was a poetry of the personal in which formerly preconceived notions of self and identity, authority and history, language and freedom were now fundamentally questioned and challenged. In the Menderes climate of violent, psychotic political paranoia the *Second New* took nothing for granted, not even meaning itself, castigating the semantic demands on the poem in a poetry that made little sense as public address.

If the *First New* was an explosion, the *Second New* was seen by many of Berk's contemporaries as a catastrophic implosion, a reckless and sui-cidal assault on the very idea of poetry itself. The poet, now distanced from society, was little more than a solipsist, babbling in a language only he could understand. Over the next three decades Berk became a fierce and outspoken defender of his own new poetry and the new poetries of Ece Ayhan, Edip Cansever, Cemal Süreya and Turgut Uyar.[2] Collectively, as the *Second New*, these poets revitalised Turkish literature, insisting, as they did, that poetry be no longer just a matter of social obligation and political commitment but a matter of personal survival, of our very existence.

"I have regarded the world," Berk once said, "as a place to write in, not to live in." Berk lived for much of his life in the Aegean town of Bodrum, known to antiquity as Halicarnassos. He was the author of more than two dozen books of poetry, as well as volumes of critical and biographical prose. He was also an acclaimed visual artist. He translated a selection of Ezra Pound's *Cantos* in 1948 and a celebrated version of

---

[2] Selected translations: Messo, G. (2009) *Ikinci Yeni: The Turkish Avant-Garde*. Shearsman Books.

Arthur Rimbaud in 1962. His awards for poetry included The Turkish Language Association Poetry Prize for *Kül* (*Ash*, 1979), the Bahçet Necatigil Prize for *İstanbul Kitabı* (*Book of Istanbul*, 1980), the 1983 Yeditepe Poetry Award for *Deniz Eskisi—Şiirin Gizli Tarihi* (*In the Sea's Wake—The Secret History of Poetry*, 1982) and the Sedat Simavi Literature Prize for *Güzelrmak* (*Beautiful River*, 1988). In 2002 Berk brought his poetic trilogy of *Ev* (*House*), *Çok Yaşasın Sayılar* (*Long Live Numbers*) and *Birşey Olanlarla Birşey Olmayanlar* (*Things That Count Things That Don't*) together under the title *Şeyler Kitabı* (*The Book of Things*, 2002), a monumental project which he described as a need "to add dust, mud, rubbish, stone, dot, dash, question mark and slug" to his "reputation as a man of small subjects." Berk's writing was a process of steady, careful refinement and, though his language never stopped changing, the vision remained remarkably clear. "The important thing," Berk tells us, "is to live the life of poetry, the writing always comes later."

George Messo
2006, 2016

1947-1975

Tree

(To Eluard)

If this sky, brought suddenly to mind, decided to grow a little more
this desperate tree
would be erased.

Kizilirmak

7 October 1951
was a cold, dark, deserted night
we were thirty people, a knife wouldn't part our lips
then we saw you from the wagon
languorously flowing
we all took out our cigarettes, lit up
and sang folk songs.

A Forest in the South

If wheat grows now in Turkey
it grows, I swear, with love.
I swear lavender, opium poppies and thyme grow, with love.
Sheep, goats, cattle
corn, rice and oats
are grown and raised in this world with love.
For thousands of years rivers run down to see the world,
so we learn for thousands of years there are rivers flowing and plants
        growing in the world's many and various parts
I talked with moss, ferns and fish
there's none that hasn't seen the world.

Now in the south if clover grows
like me it grows for a better life.
Poppies grow for this too, side by side with my roots.
If cotton opens whiter than before
its reason is the same.
I'm raised, thinking of every forest.
They too grow up thinking of all the forests,
like me, the whole of Turkey's forests.
We have reached such a point in the world's age
when no one loves the world better than anyone else,
I love the forests, rivers and hill pastures of England as much as life,
I love those of America no less.
Here water-logged rice fields, cotton and tobacco love each other no less.
Now garlic, grapevines and beans grow by embracing each other.
Now the steppes and mountains love loneliness no more,
now no one in the world loves loneliness.
Now in Iran and in Egypt and in Sudan they know why forests grow.
Now they know why veins of petrol flow
Now they know why everything in this world has life.

The Grieving Stream

Each morning my job it was
to take this plain from you
and raise it.

Each morning
my loveliest task in this world
was to magnify
                    and beautify life.

The Flower's Indescribable Grief: Yellow Crocus

We came first into the world
and as we did
we learnt to try to love.
Little did we know
we'd one day learn to mourn.

Saint-Antoine's Pigeons

I. Eleni's Hands

One day Eleni's hands come
Everything changes.
First Istanbul steps out of the poem and takes its place
A child laughs
A tree opens into flower.

Before Eleni
When I was barely a child, before I'd got used to coffee and tobacco
Even before I knew mornings or nights
I once looked at night in my hands, in my eyes
Another time morning was all around me.

Eleni comes
I'm looking at the world
That day I realise the world's not as small as it's thought
We're not as unhappy in this world as we think
That day I said we should burn all poems and start again
A new *Brise Marine*
A new *Annabel Lee*.
It's with Eleni we realize
Why this sky rose up, why it came here
With her we understand why the sea packed up and went.

One day Eleni's hands come
For the first time the sea can be seen from a street.

II. Youth

My soul
Do you hear İlhan Berk crossing the bridge?
A sparrow is slowly flying by
A fish with its head through the water is looking around
A leaf is about to fall from the branch.

Lambodis took a bottle from the shelf and opened it.
A cloud stopped in the window
Lambodis went on with his job
Cleaned his hands, sliced cucumbers, tomatoes
Then sat and pondered his youth.

It was in a house
Eleni was eighteen, Ilyadis was twenty-three
Eleni knew songs
You couldn't imagine
            Coffeehouses all over Istanbul
            Pavement cafes indoor cafes
No matter how good the songs
They never could capture Eleni.

In those days Lambodis went everywhere in Istanbul with a cigarette in
            his mouth
Eleni's most beautiful features were her hands, her garlic smelling mouth
Lambodis wasn't yet a barkeeper
Lambodis wasn't yet anything
In those days they went every Sunday to Saint-Antoine
Eleni's breasts were peeled almonds
Her hands like pigeons
Even then Lambodis' enemies were many
The whole of Istanbul was behind Eleni.

Yes,
Lambodis' youth: a leaf about to fall.
He sat by the window, watched people come and go

Come look he said to me
Look, people are going by
I watch them when I'm bored
And forget all my troubles
We forget all our troubles.

My soul, it's always the same
A man a woman doing the same thing
Soon I'll get up and go to Sirkeci
My sweetheart's leaving on a train
One day the sun won't rise, there'll be no morning,
        we fear one day it will be as if we're not in the world.

This will all come to pass, my soul
One day we'll see Istanbul is beautiful
Thereafter Istanbul is always beautiful
A long long time ago the world was much more beautiful, for example
Those clouds this sky was a place we could reach out and touch
Now they only exist in poems
It all comes down to this, my soul

This world is beautiful
And Gülhane Park is full of trees.

III. Saint-Antoine's Time of Lovemaking

This sky
Is not like this every day above Saint-Antoine
It's certainly time to make love
Windows are opened first
Ants crawl out of their nest
Mosses stir
Sky draws taut like a drum
A girl stitching in her window is happy for the first time
Homes and coffeehouses facing the sea are happy for the first time
For now Lambodis has nothing to fear
Eleni has nothing to fear
The pigeons will all take flight and no one will know fear
An hour when everything wakes
Love will begin
Everything will stop
A girl's hand stretching out to her dress will stop
Saint-Antoine will rise from his sarcophagus and walk off to a place on
        the coast
With him tombs and holy relics, Jesus himself will follow on behind
In everything's place there will be love
Chairs
Windows
Saint-Antoine's ceiling will walk straight to another ceiling
A door straight to another door
Nothing will want to be smaller
You'll see the sky grow large
The sea more blue
This love will go from eye to eye like a dark complexion
Going now to Istanbul along with all the best songs
Now, no matter where, a girls hand, her mouth, grow for this
For this a child clings to its mother's breast
Saint-Antoine's pigeons
Fly for this
The anxiety of order in poetry is for this
This sky can have no other meaning.

IV. Childhood in Fener

Saint-Antoine's childhood
Was spent in Fener

He's just started going to church
The first picture he sees is Jesus' lemon coloured face
The slender legs.
A cloud caught in the window
A child a little older than he is praying
The entire mass of saints suddenly passes before his eyes
The candle falls from his hand.
In those days Antoine's father was a shoemaker in Karaköy
He loved God as he loved his hammer and anvil
In those days it rained every day in Istanbul

One day he stops in front of Hagia Dikolas' sarcophagus
Who knows how much the sea is missed, he thought
A window opens
They look at the sea
Then he goes home
And explains it all.

Childhood in Fener:
First contact with the sea.

V. Morning

Saint-Antoine recalls a morning
Like mornings which brought with them Ilyadis' songs.
One morning he gathers himself and enters the street
Gazing at shop windows, sky, cinema posters
I am with the new morning for the first time, he says to himself
The first time encountering sea
The first time with poetry.
That day, the whole day, he watches the street
He draws children indoors and talks about improbable things
There is no God, for example, he says
Later together they walk over the bridge
First he says hello to the sea
Then he returns to his place
He sees all the saints have awoken and washed their faces
There is something about this
Saints work like all of us
Some clean windows
Some carry water.

That day there is no evening
Morning never ends.

VI. Eleni Light

One morning Saint-Antoine goes to Iaos Yokios
Night descends on the journey.
Suddenly he remembers Fotini Nermeroğlu
        and goes to Fotini Nermeroğlu's house.
His Holiness Saint-Antoine is here, says Fotini
The whole of Zürefa Street proffers coffee from its windows
The girls hastily cover their breasts with their hands
Elpiniki gazes at the stars and everything's in its rightful place
Marvido Apiyos, Eftelya and Hagia Feya, Hagia Dikolas followed by
        Galata Tower, enormous Yüksekkaldirim and Eleni's mouth as
        beautiful as this world all follow on into Fotini's house.
Saint-Antoine looks at the world, "The world's not all that bad, Fotini
        Nermeroglu's not bad at all," he says to himself.
He asks for a Bible
They give him one.
He takes it, crosses out here and there, writes it anew.
Teo Fano, Maneli, Avi Antimos and Kalina step down off a cloud
Salome is on her knees
No, says Antoine at first, there are no longer such things, he says
He raises Salome to her feet
He holds out a Bible to Kalina
From now on, he says, this is the Bible.

Eleni's groin suddenly radiates light
The universe is suddenly sparkling.

VII. Sky

A cloud above Istanbul
White cloud yellow cloud black cloud

5 in the morning
not a sound in Saint-Antoine
what did he do, this man asks
then he answers himself
when we were all asleep
he stole the sky.
What can we do
but hang him.

Ha ha
Ha ha

What do the crowds have to say,
For three days we can't pray
There is no sky

My soul snapped the rope,
the sky is about to fall

What a strange thing this sky
like a handkerchief
we didn't think it would fit in a pocket.

The crowds stir
Who will pull the rope?
Someone says something
calls out

It's nothing

That day there is no evening
Morning never ends.

Arma Virumque Cano
(Virgil)

I. Saturday Darkness

We will walk a thousand years
first we will enter a street

a Genoese will bring me news of you
I will wait for you naked

they see us from Hagia Sophia
there is no one who does not see

Saturday darkness
stares at the Polish church

we waited for a thousand years
we are together first in a poem.

Discarding their cloths to the night
they will run to the Sultan with news of us.

I can't say I will ever see you again
and we never see each other again.

II. Ramparts

You descend from royalty.
Me, I know nothing of empires.
One day we'll see, we're in the bazaar
there's Constantine VI, Saint Leo's hand, Jesus' sandals, that something-
        face in the bazaar
the Goth's obelisk and Balikli Monastery's suns there before the houses.
Istanbul had not yet fallen, what wonderful fish they fried
Istanbul just wouldn't fall.

We withdraw all the money minted in our name and won't mint more.
We take neither Beato Majano's nor Paolo Belini's medallions, we return
      them all.
Ramparts are of no use to us, nobody needs ramparts
Look, it's true, no one needs such things.
Your people built more than enough ramparts
and we've had more than enough grief.

Istanbul will never see me again.

III. Little

One morning we woke and found all the gates locked and all the streets
      held.
We didn't take this easily.
Now I suppose the streets will no longer stop and start somewhere
      without you.
Without you a window won't open and the sea come to a halt before
      your house,
nor the rain suddenly think of pouring.
I don't know where you'd go if you go.
Maybe it's good in Byzantium, maybe bad, or maybe I can't tell.
I don't like streets without small shops and cafes, nor do I like the rooms
and walls.
I can't stand kings.
Let's say what you said is true, let's say you were first into the street,
No barbecues, no frying fish.
You're in a street,
all the things I said were absent, green lettuce, quinces, the warmth of
      destitution,
a heap of things that never come to man on a day that will never come,
so there you are in such a place
Constantine VI has bequeathed all waters to you.
This does not change the universe.
This is not it.

IV. Map of the Firmament

One night we are in the vast blackness of the sky.
At night, gazing at the entire sky
Saint Paustrolls around in his underwear
Constantine thinks only of the world
and here Leo II is more lonely than ever.
A galleon moves slowly past,
water is everywhere, at a standstill.
There is nothing at all in the sky,
a pity so many men are bored.

One day you and I see this together
One day you are not there, that day there is nothing.

V. The Gate of Ahmet I

Overwhelming convoys of fire, slaughter, death and tyrannies.
In such a night you call out to me.
Enough, you say, of this wrack and ruin, this enmity,
        let them end at the gate of Ahmet I and rear their heads no more.
Let us not know murder.
Take one step and an unending unshrinkable chasm opens before us.
Fires solve nothing, massacres put nothing right.
Look how far I am from you yet nothing is changed.
Our waking one morning spoils nothing, puts nothing on track.
Only love plucks me from my place, carries me to unknown parts.
We travelled long and so we came to our end.

At the gate of Ahmet II
ground was taken again.

VI. Invitation

Don't call for me I can see you.
I'll put out these fires and come.

Water Days I

Water

is looking for you,
comes even
to your feet.

Water Days II

I

was water long ago,
Thales
is my source.

Water Days III

The pebble

thinks
you
are water.

Water Days IV

A praying mantis
a hill
come and go

on the water's surface.

Water Days V

At the city gate
stands a puddle
as if
not of this world.

Water Days VI

        I

                    am water

leave me

        let me run.

Season of the Hunt

Prologue

(O you! And O tea-time.) The house is woken. Halayik pours tea. The hand drops sugar into tea. Handfuls. Bedevi winds the clock. The Bey's slender bridge sways. *The castle gate creaks. One girl wakes another.*

> *…and the Bey leans forward and kisses you. The house gently sways and is gone.*

> *The child lets go of his paper boats. Returns, waits for tea.*

> +

> *The face sails far away.*

I

The Hunt

The men go hunting. Hold birds in their hands. The women are silent, waiting for the men. The men return with flowers. Swans gaze at the men returning from the hunt. Fires burn. The women sit, listening to a book being read. Birds and flowers listen too. A peacock stands motionless, as if in a painting. A casement window is opened from inside, closed from inside. Later a man comes and teaches the women arithmetic. (In those days women knew arithmetic.) A dog watches them, then leaves. Then the cavalrymen come. No one thinks about the war. War is a kind of loneliness. It enters not a single house. The girls have hands and feet. The Jew sits before a bookrest, a girl comes in. One girl looks at the other girls. The men are holding the women's hands. All the women's faces are long,

> a long
> slender face
> enters painting.

In those days there are no Americans. Women wear underwear. I begin a bawdy poem but can't finish it.

Later,
> women are in paintings. No one goes into houses. No one goes out for the hunt. Though they do return. A book remains always open. A window is closed to the sky,

(we see it all).

II

The Women

First it is the women who meet him. First a woman firms up her breasts, then all the women firm up their breasts.

The men fall asleep.

I used to play. I'd run my hand over the edge of his mouth. Two rowing boats slid into the sea. Then we'd sit and watch them. A woman washes herself beside us. I wash her too. I take her lines and leave. The woman holds you by the hips. She bangs against doors. Slender.

Outside they race a horse
     pure white
       and let it go.

+

Sometime later it returns.
Black.

III

The Rampart

(a)

Upstairs is loneliness. Rampart closes in on rampart. Closes in on sheep, silk, Arabian red. The merchant puts down his silks and leaves. Embroidery frames are stretched. The girls' slender faces take form. A boy with a thousand locks of hair holds the rampart gate. Musicians enter. They twist their moustaches for the Sultan.

The islands remain far away.

A piece of silk falls into the water. Three Beys laugh. We're surprised.

(b)

The Queen descends,
    ancient.
With her
    something else
yellow
like love.

IV

The Child

(The women were left downstairs.)
Grapes were harvested. A tall child
                              placed
                              his foot on ours.

(Trees, and water crossing water. The black servant fetches the mirror,
the needle box. The sheep's fleece is sheared and combed. A woman makes
love to a balcony. Galleons arrive.)

From China.

She opens a book and reads. She glances from a window out through
another. A black servant passes with a painting. Sleep leans against a
balcony.

+

The child goes always by a canal.

V

The Men

…and the men take whatever is there and join the fleet. Then the Sultan comes in. (Suddenly I see your hands are different.) The Sultan crosses his legs and sits down. Your own feet disappear. Night disappears too.

Later, that tall
handsome
man
takes you. You.

The Sultan continues to sit. He stares. (A Copt leaves, caressing the cord.) That man doesn't leave you. He laughs. The feet you possess rest against my sky, feet that never were yours. The Sultan leaves. The fleet pauses. Perhaps he never stands. The Sultan. Too weak. And so as not to bore him the rope climbers, bridges, tents, those who twirl dishes in the air never leave, and never stop. *Wherever can I take you? Wherever is there? Perhaps a blood-soaked severed hand inside a carriage. Perhaps they're firing on the galley ships and castles in our absence.*

And the Sultan stands up. (The buses stop.)

VI

Upstairs a woman takes a woman's mouth in her mouth.

VII

Flow

The baby is laid out. As if it had just been born. Some water is released at first. Copious. Slippery. Slides towards other water. Then it spreads out like a jellyfish, embraces the other water. The water becomes rough, and stays so. Then for some reason changes, as if washed with soap.

Lifeless, it falls.

The girls pass by. The men avert their eyes. They too pass without stopping. The yellow stain remains on the wooden floor and won't come off.

+

I pick up one of the children and go.

VIII

Me

Downstairs they carry a white cross. The child Muhammed is laughing out of the walls. Chora feeds the birds from on top of her beautiful, black camel. Houses of three and four floors. Arched, small, with neither windows nor walls. Yellow balconies. And white beds. (In every epoch beds are white. In our time too they are white.) There is much weeping. Winter sherbets are brought and rosewater sprinkled. The donkeys and camels are awesome. An Arab gathers the girls and strips them. The girls cover their breasts. In a picture Zeus kidnaps Europa, then rapes her. (How beautifully the man holds the book of stories. Angels came but didn't descend.)

And in secret rooms they make love. The women admit no one and make love. Having grown, they move down to the bedroom. Our white sides attract them. Perhaps it is your hands they love.

I am weak. I can't stand. I stare. I look and I am weak. I wear a new crescent shirt. The horses wait at the gate, as always.

Having grown you go downstairs.
Having grown from my looking.

+

I leave.

IX

Sefine

One night the hunting ends. Sefine comes out. The galleons come to a halt. Three Beys step off their horses. With them part-ridges, falcons, mountebanks. Cartridges, the whole fleet. (A man makes the corpse laugh.) The Queen takes a pheasant and leaves. Then men hand out the dead game. Boys light fires. And women leave a paper-light wind in their wake. The galley stops. Copper trays of halva come in. The dead game stinks. We leave the sky. Suddenly the house fills and then recedes. The tents come down. A man puts down the game. *What a beautiful child is the hunted animal. Its naked feet.*

I set the galley aflame. I'm there with the smell of fresh meat. The meat withdraws and waits. The copper pans and rice are still. Girls come for the birds. They cross over the canal. They hold their hands to the fire and keep them there.

You climb continuously up and down a ladder.

The hunt rises.

X

Epilogue

(O you! And O...) The dead bring in the night. We look on. The black servant lights the lamp. Girls come out. The horse doesn't rear. The corpse grows pale. Sky enters. Rolls up carpets. Calls out to the girls. A hand closes the page. *Voices go downstairs. Wander around the house, come in, then make off with the water jug.*

It remains yellow. The nail cutter comes, clips the dead Sultan's finger-nails and toenails.

The corpse is bored. Gives the carnation a shove.

Me, I go down a canal.

Paris, 1964

You

I looked you over. Your voice, old and alone
I undressed you. Your plentiful mouth.

I take in your eyes. Your eyes
are the Middle Ages. Vast and uninhabited.

I take hold of your hands and say white,
your pale white naked flesh, your loins.

I part your loins. Your scent
is the scent of sky and of trees.

I lay down and claim your voice
your voice! Istanbul. Elgin. Eternal.

We emerge onto a steep rampart. I dismount
from my horse. I'm white. You're white.

Epilogue

Later I spent the whole day strolling around
I wrote this poem, maybe you heard.

Istanbul

A small, flat rectangle. And a heading: *Istanbul, 1574; Braun-Hogenberger. Gravuré.*

A subscript. Below the picture, centred in Gothic lettering: BYZANTYUM LUNC CONSTANTINOPOLIS (or so I read it). Clearly from Hogenberger's own hand. Piece by piece he begins to weave the picture: sets down lines, triangles, rectangles. Ups perpendiculars. Attractive. Autonomous. Establishing Hogenberger's own alphabet, transformed into the great vocabulary of ISTANBUL. On wood. A gravure, then, to be scoured out with a steepen. Repeatedly looking at the lithograph. Given by a Galata Jew. He sensed the soul of a Bohemian engraver in Hogenberger (*long time seller of mulberries and figs. A bit of a mapmaker too, as a man who had travelled around. He lives at the Guild. These days he works on wood. At night he spreads before him pictures of Istanbul. The seven hills. The plains. The valleys. The reinforced walls. As in this engraving. This engraving: isn't this the point I want to come to? Could this prologue have any other meaning? Like all prologues it is an addition and unnecessary. But impossible without it. Think of all those masters! Which has saved himself from them? And entered straight upon the subject? Like those beautiful textbooks. Simple and direct. A table of contents on the first page, in bold print, geometrically placed one below the other. Which is fine, but why don't we come straight to the point? Without long-winded words. And with a rough outline of the subject. And without delving into history? For instance, to say it's a peninsula*).

A peninsula. Imitating a triangle. Three-dimensional. Horizontal and distended. Rising to a peak. And drawing a line at the Golden Horn. And descending to bays and islands. To a continent. From three sides and up above. Because this is a bird's eye view.—*And it shall remain so*. Completing itself with a straight 18 miles. With its inlets and promontories. It will close in and straighten its peaks. From seven points, silent and steep. Entering roads and streets. Crossing a long, narrow strait. To die in a sea commemorated in Greek letters. With a marginal note: TÜRKELI. Three seas (it's always how maps of Istanbul are seen, from a bird's eye view). And there it rests in bays with its S's and U shapes. Then returns again to itself. Again leaving islands—like outstretched feet. Throwing out arms like an octopus. To reproduce there, separate from its body. And old men: in the courtyards of mosques, holding children's hands. Sleeping with children, their beautiful mouths. And dark. And Imperial (that's how Hogenberger approached it too: dark and full of sorrow). That's why he engraves using black dyes, black ink. On wood. Veinless. Smooth. Drying in the sun. The grease still seeps out. And now it is slippery under his hand. Walnut. Different from itself. Because that's how it has always lived. Those migrants, those fires, have served no other use than to augment its loneliness. That's why it's Türkeli, the land of the Turks. Straight and calm. And still like that. Those ramparts were not built for nothing: two floors high and steep. For all of this, lonely and by itself. Right-facing, protruding. As far as they can be on this engraving. Indistinct. Since the city appears on paper it will leave its name, and that of Hogenberger, to history. Even if Pera and Galata slowly become transparent. With its 12 gates. Its tower of Christ. And its Latin inscriptions. Since he's making a picture he should use shadows. Dark, light, even lighter. Always taking notes. Measuring proportions like all mapmakers. It's a picture-map he makes. Isn't it clear from the roads' contours? With their black, curved lines. The sea left white. And the Bosphorus. A peninsula then.

That's why he scours. The thought of a picture: for a monograph. Contemporary. He has thought of our times. Peppered his engraving with portraits of the sultans: Orhan, Murat I, Beyazit I, Mehmet I, Murat II, Selim the Grim, Beyazit II. With Mehmet the Conquerer in the centre. Long-faced and bearded. Larger than althe rest. Only Süleyman the Magnificent on horseback. Dark, with large eyes. (*You know Süleyman the Magnificent: wide-browed and short-legged. Unsmiling. That's why he never used concubines. He used face-powder and mascara.*) Three horsemen clear the way. Armed. They look ahead. And obstruct the front of Tophane, in a circle. Full face and in profile. In quilled and crested turbans. Past Venetian made galleys (*is he not Venetian himself? Of German origin. From Aksoy. He never leaves Galata. For that is where he is looking from. The sun on his back, pencil in hand*). Now we see the Imperial mosques one by one. All speaking the same language. An agile tongue. Extending in width towards the top. Like a well-finished quatrain. Only the houses rise and the waterside residences descend. And they do. Always with a steel pencil, scratching his signature. Now he returns to Langa. He longs for the sea. But first he stops at Karaköy. Now he engraves children's voices. Carves out a bird. Lifts out a fish etc. It's the turn of Istanbul grasses now. He works in a leaf, then a cypress, as an old inhabitant of Üsküdar. He raises up a tombstone. Draws Balkapan Inn with a thick line, so it stays within its frame. But it doesn't. He wanders off to Seven Hills.

He rubs past the Tower of Almenas. Leaves the Ramparts of Theodosia on the right. Now he rests beside a cross. In his hand a yellowed figure of Jesus. He kisses it. And again he engraves battle walls and summer palaces. He stops in front of a waterside house. With two doors. Dark. To have a better look at Seraglio Point and at Topkapi. A city. 699,000m². A ceiling: domed, in mother-of-pearl. A long eulogy. Guards. Thick, stone walls. Four rectangles. One inside the other. As if a rising Tower of Babel. Wooded. Tasselled guards: colliding with a galley. Finally into the Hippodrome. A pentagonal shape, head in hand with John the Evangelist. To gaze at the palace birds? Or the Egyptian obelisk? With its copper sphere. Noted in Neshri's history. Now he willl ook out of a coffeehouse window. His cross dangling. His eyes fixed on Süleymaniye mosque. Its great courtyard. And four corners. And there he lingers, drinking tea. Melling's engraving in his hand (*or is that what I say, thinking of Melling. Dear Melling! And Selim III, who never could leave birdshops and spice-shops alone. Wearing a stambouline*). Now where is he? At Yüksekkaldirim? Hagia Nicolas? The Thousand-and-one columns? (or else). He turns his face to Hagia Sophia. Bolt upright. A straight line. It breaks at Petrios Gate. Into the shape of a *tughra*, an Ottoman seal. After a while he will go down to the coast, reading a map by Piri Reis, stopping often on his way.

According to Asagik and Lazarus, an island. Full of ins and outs, and Armenians. With inner fortifications 20 feet thick. Outer walls of 10 feet. 225 turrets. Caucasian horsemen. Andreas, first bishop. John, a saint. Stakis, who wrote him a greeting. Macedonius, first consul. Photius, the last patriarch. Hagia Irene, a church (not seen). John, a Baptist and gout-ridden like Mehmet the Conqueror. Rosario, a virgin. Michael, emperor. Hydraulis, an aqueduct. Khrisi Pili, a building. Hovannesian, a moneylender (*from Pera. Sleeps in his shop. A follower of Lazarus. And, like Ahmet I, he hates the number 14*). Ayvansaray's suburbs with its 17 Jewish districts. Gothic columns. Obelisks. Horses and donkeys. And Inns. This is why it's an island. But it will also be an engraving. On wood. It tangles around houses, walls, books, strikes metals, iron, zinc, goes out with women. But will always remain on wood. To die there. Always to be Istanbul. Around 1574. Or a morning? And today. This hour. Unchanged. In its law of motionlessness. Then it will return to its wall. Its origin, an engraving. With its Theodosian moats. As it is:

Berk-like. And

he stops. Because he's at Galata. A district. With two steep slopes. With ditches and curves. They're filling in the sea. An Arab blocks his view. Night is announced in Latin. Chains are drawn. And its 12 gates. Its bitter waters. 146 steps. Its sleepless monasteries. And Voyvodas. Its squares. Its Latin church. The embossed silver icon of Mary, made by Lucas. Sent to Pulcheria by Theodosus the Younger's wife Eudoxia, which Pulcheria always carried by her side. Mary, who appeared to two blind men at Hagia Dicolas where they regained their sign but never saw her again. Surrounded by battlements. Venetian and Pisan. Where the bowmen were placed. There, to live in the towers 47 years, 13 days and 5 hours.

But let us again return to the engraving. And to Hogenberger. And let's describe whatever we see. In the first person. And the present tense. The closest and quickest path to reality (because it starts with I see). Therefore: O my eyes! You should start because I see a road, far off. Winding towards Psamathia along the city-wall. Aren't there a lot of walls? You say. Could it be any other way? Now that it's the entrance to a road, it must be closed. By wind. Medieval. So, what else do you see? Hills? Cut out by sky. It's true, we'd forgotten the sky. Like on a pirates map, one that never leaves Istanbul. Yes, that sky you see. With its Byzantine face. Was seen by Constantine the Great (*they say he was blonde. And very frightened. Because he had lived long. He wore scarlet robes, feared the Goths, loved the Visigoths. Bronze. Wood and stone*). And stop. Taking this engraving in your hand. Torn from a book and spread on the poet's table. He keeps looking at it, lighting his pipe. Every morning. In Atal City (a terrible sentence but I won't cross it out). As he dresses. For a life: a place in which to wander, with Crusaders. A life, then. So let's stop. And end this. With parentheses—it's better this way. Wasn't this how we began? Then we should continue thus. With a parallel to the prologue. Without summary. Without annotation. Without "O"s—wringing the neck of poeticism. So there you are.

This Caesar weighed the land.

from **Woodcuts**

Steppe

Get ready now
from here on not a single tree to be seen.

Yeşilyurt Street

This is all the street saw:
a man unloading a wagon
a passing child
a woman watching them both.

Country Life

A hair tent.
Three chickens.
All for a country life.

Sunset

Sunset. Silently falls
below the plain.

—I drive birds into the sky.

Sun

Sun comes out, takes up its watercolour set.
Sits on the rooftop.

Repeats itself.

Autumn III

Autumn putting on its sock
—for a journey?

Picture

In dry grass
two horses graze,
a woman hangs laundry on a line.

Unknowingly, they magnify the plain.

Window

A yellowed samovar
and a white handkerchief,

as though a window.

Plane Tree Leaf

Who knows what this leaf of the plane tree inspires
in a poet with ten books to his name.

1978-1982

The Thames

I

Turner sketches the Thames. A northern tributary. Ash smelling.

Was Turner tall? He loved long rivers and the Thames.

Sky like mud.

And Death slowly strolls around as if laying eggs
waving to the Thames from a hill
(as if readying for winter
                              or for pain).

The Mersey and Humber rivers flow

slowly Thames keels are toyed

a clock strikes three at a crossroads

a cormorant flies in and flies off
a man is selling spermaceti candles
and sticking a stamp on his letter.

It's 1962, I'm in a house in Elsworthy working on a history of a river,
a river as thick as a grammar book and as old as a Genoese sledgehammer
in Galata.

At night I'm out to Piccadilly sitting on a stone
          flushing a pigeon into flight
I break a glass with a black man in a bar and stare
          long and hard at a woman, at a twisting road and
I take up the Thames and go, then perhaps it's another river, the Bosphorus
(so it's the Bosphorus and Asafpasha mansion, its divans and delicate curtains
a canary—from the Philippines, yellow, it never sings or else the
canary
          I'm looking at
is a window—the interiors of dark rooms, lanterns, kitchen hands
          (mostly Armenian), the men's room, frying pans, plates,
          knives and forks and lamps, fuses, maces, brazier coals,
          administrators, the little woman, a key, robes and jackets,
Louis XIV broadcloth shawls and chairs
and a ferry with twin propellers, a round sternpost—and a French kitchen
          top
older than death
in the middle of July).

Perhaps too a fish, a sword fish—obstinate, dumb—and bluefish and
        mackerel
or else nothing at all.

But I keep a diary in a park and write BOREDOM ten times in a notebook
(a book you bought one morning from Şişhane hill from a man whose hands
        spent hours crafting the book
his strange face
that now appears on the full page)
and I stare at a red carnation in the lapel of a passing Englishman
and geraniums.

Here the Thames is like the Danube
thin skinned
and like the timid Golden Horn on the Orthodox shore
and howls in the night in a language I've never heard
with its counter currents and darkness
like a white woman's waking face.

Suddenly I lose her trail at Abbey. She: the Thames. Maybe she's entered
   a lokanta.
Cooled some food. Looked out from a window. Listened to a kettle boiling
   on a stove. Watched its steam rising. Wondering why its water
   boils. And thought about the days of the week: Monday Tuesday
   Wednesday Thursday Friday Saturday Sunday. How bored God
   is on a Sunday. His wearing a cravat. How it rained so slowly
   that day. How the wind limped around. How the sun withdraws
   into its room. How she'd closed the curtains and read poems not
   wanting anyone to see. And then the sun's light.—Sunlight: *I'm
   here! I'm here!* It said—Perhaps she got lost with a boy from the
   palace, I say. She washed the threshold of a house. Or greeted T.S.
   Eliot in Trafalgar Square. And maybe flowed in and out of The
   Waste Lands. Studied physical education. Practised gymnastics.
   Stretched out her arms and legs. Considered her length. Found
   her width. Worked out the mean. Multiplied. Passed beyond her
   tributaries. Wrote that down too. Passed onward to Greenwich
   and Blackwell.

She sat down or thought first of the seas. Absorbed China. And Ceylan,
   Malta,
Jamaica, the Bahamas, Bermuda, Gibraltar, Canada.

Later Australia, New Zealand, India and Africa and the crown republics
   (*reminders of*
botanicnexiles—H.G. Wells) and the British Navy and the Ancient
   History of the Assyrians and a fur-trade centre, Hudson Bay
   Company and other companies, rail networks and steam ships
   and two places of exile and a bundle of possessions and Defoe
   and Fielding's satires.

And then our own: Namik Kemal riding a horse to the theatre, Sultan
        Aziz and his
garter and Ziya Pasha, behind them prisoners doing hard labour and
        women and men's hats and slavery and bulls and horses and The
        History of Work and John Locke, Jesus of Nazareth & the saying:
        itiseasierforacameltopassthroughtheeyeofaneedlethanforarichmanto
        enterthekingdomofheaven! And the 1st and 2nd International and a
        muddy-footed-giant (by the name of Imperialism) and her own
        dirty history

Edwards the I, II and III

The Commonwealth and male sex organs

                                        (the first birds with mammals)

Then she strips off as in the days of Rome. Hangs up her robes.
        My 160 miles! She says. Looks at a picture on the wall. Her
        own picture. A river like a snake. And twisted. Curling upward
        towards the city. Going down at Limehouse. To the West Indies.
        And stops to look at herself passing St. Paul's Cathedral. Coming
        as far as Bow Church. Then stretching out around St. Dunstan.
        Crossing over

                                                        (and)

Strolls around at Customs House. Spins a barrel with a fisherman. They go in and out
of houses. She seizes hold of a crucifix, a window. They head towards Oxford Street (you know Oxford Street). She bought a banana. Drank a bottle of milk. And said: *It's evening!* And as she stopped two swallows passed each other in flight. First she sent a man on his way to St. Paul's (*I need to go to Hungry. You should ready yourself, I'm passing the Danube!*) At Hyde Park paper fell from her pockets. And there she sat with a Scot.

Then she strikes Blackfriars Bridge and goes on to Bankside.

Criss-crosses up a small rise and gains the centre with a fisherman
passes through stations, winches, the smell of leather. Throws out her fishing line
and she comes to a stop beside a piece of Staffordshire porcelain.

II

Is this the morning of 1962? Overcast. Foggy.
A face like Queen Victoria—always gazing off at a distance
and always using her left hand
she never placed her hands on chairs
which is why she always woke at night and changed the water of her
        geraniums
and hash plant—

and morning, always that morning on the road to Hanley. Hasty with
        small feet
but St. George is peevish and at Rotten Row
she enters a church without taking off her shoes. And never sits

and is jealous of Jesus.

And June is about to fall on the river
and sweet chestnut trees

and a child spins a wheel in a shop and says I haven't slept since last night

and a girl sizes up dantella and tülle to a curtain edge. Her face like paper.

And a man is kneading dough in a bakery and can only read the *Manifesto*
      in dialect

and there is a watch with a flywheel in the shape of a question mark near
      Harwich

and the sun is shown with a giant U and the water is 4 + 4

and the water-mill on the banks of the Mosel River is as it was in the time
of the great Karl
a fountain pen
and cotton paper still comes from China to Middle Gardner Street
and to Temple
and to Dombart
Roundtown takes a right at Dombart, takes the night and washing on a
      line.

At St. Petrus again I lose and then re-find the Thames.
And every morning God appears in the form of a glass of water
dresses and goes out into Elsworthy Street looking for a friend
and takes a magnetic needle from the Arabs and gives it to the
            Europeans in 1180
and eyeglasses to Florenza
and uses bonds
lights up London Street in the XV century
makes pocket watches tick and birds eat grapes
Is carbon an acid? She later asks. If not it's eternal, she says.
Then lifts the lid on Nature's Dialectics
proclaims the immortality of Protein
and turns her head towards the Thames
(Thames: *Where am I?* She thinks)
counting the bridges to herself
moves off towards Greenwich. Sets her watch.
Is detained at Blackwell, seeks out docks, enters and comes out of a canal
crosses to a small island, lingers around houses
(and again thinks of Australia, India, Africa, islands, the Caribbean,
Cretan
            oils, broad beans, dill,
                    and finally comes right to now)

   God is in the service of the English! She says. And lies down.

And the wind's arm falls.

A Street Leads Down to the Sea

I

Belgrade, like an old face on the wall. I'm looking
at Belgrade on the wall.

Men are climbing a rampart
a sailboat goes by.

Five thousand years earlier I'm disembarking
with the Celts, our Celts. A Celtic soup,

saltless and oily. Celt. Long whiskered,
blonde, blue-eyed.

              Celt. From the mountains
and with a thousand-page book like the Bible.

II

              Mihaila.
I'm walking through Mihaila.

Three girls pass by a street,
in the air three question marks remain.

In Gajava a woman lights two candles
I change the candles' place.

III

Sabrona Crekva. Jesus, dark and dejected.
I seize his open hands.

A street leads down to the sea—
is there a Serbian night in the street?

Three men are going up 29 November Street: me,
I'm tramping down Zeleni Venac with my three day beard.

Paris

The Seine divides Paris, pouring nowhere and to no death

Gare de l'Est, long like a winter's day and smelling of trees,
Shabby as a pilchard and full of noise

A man brushes his moustaches. He's as yellow as a Chinaman

A beech tree is writing silence and February in *Haussmann*

The Cardinal coffeehouse smells of wild thyme and old inlay
And bankers (did bankers wash corpses years ago and still weep for it?)

Gramont Street is in the hand of the wind
Clearly it wants to be with God to sit in cafés, take morning strolls
Then takes stamps from the hands of an aged philatelist
To cross the Seine, go to *Saint-Germain* and sit in Lipp's
Then draw pictures on pavements, dance to a kasap air

And then return

Does this street lead to Montparnasse? Or to a shop selling wild herbs
          and silent
voiceless flowers
And a denizen of the Red Sea who slept with a woman—someone
muttering,
          wandering through the streets of Alexandria,
Who woke startled one morning in autumn in a small coffeehouse, next
          to him a bottle of olive oil and loneliness. Boulevard Haussmann
          stretches far away and a man,
The Song of Maldoror under his arm
and de Sade. Wizen-faced like an Eskimo, walking alone, waking alone
          on the hotel's
fifth floor.
Brews tea. One who listens to the life of creaking wood
Wanders always underground
and does not wash

So there it is about to turn past *Notre-Dame* and the night

And the Île-Saint-Louis (or a white house: "playing old Macedonian
          thieves' songs
that start out with the line—*If only I were in your bed now!*

And fixing his eyes on Crete, as if photographing the sun,

And copying monastic rules at night and wandering with a forest in his
          pocket").

The Seine thins out at Saint-Michel. And beds down
At Charenton like a shy student in his dorm

At the Pont de Sèvres like a bandit's den

As young as paper announcing births

And filthy mid-July

Stroking pre-pubescent moustaches, and the dark rue *Condé*

Leads to the Odéon and is as lonely as a breadcrumb

Two women pass by and they have never heard of the Marquis de Sade
And azaleas

An Austrian girl's face is listening to Bach
And so are the slender hands of a poet

And a boy goes past carrying a freshwater fish he's caught

Rue Danton is like a brushed tooth

And your face
Your face like a pen found on the coast
Like an unending gulf-stream undertow
And with that rugged
Face of yours I climb *Sacré-Coeur*

Your hands grow small, you don't know where to put them
And your voluminous mouth, except on the whitest of days

Is this rue Cujas? Where you strolled with an Algerian who kept his money
        in a pouch,
Carried a knife, had an amber cigarette-holder and a face the size of a hand

In Cluny you look at a Book of Hours (A man is picking wheat/ a thin
        stream flows
under a thin bridge/ A woman's mouth waves goodbye from her chateau/
        A stopped water clock/ And I climb a hideously long road)

A student charms a snake in the Place de l'Étoile
His face like a painting
He blows his nose loudly as I pass, bends and pulls up his boots

Paris is like a box. The inclined head of a violin. To the left, yet again,
    the Louvre and Charles V. The Bastille? The Bastille is unseen.
    So—Louis XIV has not yet said, 'I am the law!' And Charles
    V hasn't yet grown a moustache. *And yellow dye had not been
    found. Organs were played with water. The post horse is about to
    come in, so too the fob watch and fireworks, the musket and the
    pedal piano. And the temperature scale. But the rectangle was
    already known.* The Tuileries like the Louvre's right arm. And
    this leads to a square by Saint-Honoré. And there's no one there.
    Hubert Robert's wife is waiting for the street lamps. Half of
    Saint-Germain is visible. A street crosses Richelieu. A man gets
    into a carriage. The Place de Carousel is long and never sees
    the Seine. They work with ropes as in the time of Louis XV.
    Will we wait for Louis XV's time to see the sky and Pont-Neuf?
    And salted herrings (herrings were salted in the Thirteenth
    Century—Engels), Sainte-Chapelle, L'arbre de mai and the Tour
    de l'Horloge. Earth hollowed, chasmed, canyoned. A destitute
    woman gouging holes in a door post. And Voltaire's face. (I'm
    in rue Nazarin. In a small restaurant with a black man He stares
    constantly ahead of himself. Perhaps he's thinking of a poem
    which has two meanings in Chinese. Or else he's undressing a
    woman on the third floor of a hotel, a woman who always lived
    alone, who writes the word 'winter' in an ancient script, whose
    hands assume a pose no longer used. With short eyelashes,
    a moustache and a signet ring. She's probably turning into
    Solférino now. Buying kerosene as she passes the oil yard, the
    ironworks, the carpenters, the flint-makers. And she peels off her
    clothes, crushes garlic, mixes it with herbs

and sees me for the first time)

Is this crowd welcoming Henri II? Or does it welcome rain always slanting
        through a poem?

The sun moved to the right side of the Eiffel Tower. Put on its corpse.
        Withdrew

The Île-Saint-Louis, like a glass of water,

As if revealing the wide arc of death

Like the coping stone of a building

Suddenly I take your mouth into mine like a desolate rose
It is as if mounting a white horse
We gallop past trees timber bridges

Saint-Denis is like thuluth script

I breathe in lung-fulls of frankincense in a Greek church

Your face is waxy. I am thinking of a rhyme for your face

Sainte-Clotilde stands motionless

And I think the Eiffel Tower is the longest of shadows
And the Pont de Sully

Franco, assassin! A man writes in chalk on a wall
And a crucifix falls upon the day

The bells of Sainte-Clotilde ring out unceasingly

My bed is cold. I work on a poem *Season of the Hunt*. And I say to myself
        one day
I must write the rooftops of Paris
And then its sky

The sky over Saint-Jacques is like an unfamiliar poem
And at Versailles and Chartres it never was

Noises coming from Les Invalides. And a bird is weaving silence into the air
I say again, I must write these Paris rooftops.
Then the fruit market. Sundays in Paris. Its butcher's wives. Of Cihat
Burak. Of Güzin's face
And its city walls.

Saying all this I duck into a street
Paris is like a fleet of steamships
And sadness is the best rhyme I've found

Evening arrived over Pigalle in Sunday clothes. Went in and out of shops.

Wandered around in rue Cauchois. Wore pink shirts. Stretched out.

Now we wander the streets together. The fourth floor of a house.
In a room.

A mason and I hold a plumb line in Concorde

The sky is about to fall in Montmartre

We call in on a student who writes one of Nâzım's poems in a notebook

We bandage an injured worker. Together we close and open a shop.

À bas toutes les dictatures! a girl screams out

And the wind gathers up the leaves in the Luxembourg Park
And Paris is like a striker's face near the Sorbonne

And children children children the sky falling

Sofia

In Alexander Nevski church a woman strolls with her kids
as though in a garden. Two men are praying.

Standing like a black candle a priest stares at me
his face the colour of lemon, his slender hands yellow.

I walk, hands in pockets. Voices from Ruski Boulevard—
is it a woman calling from window to window?

Or a rose, I wonder, falling into morning?
I set my watch to the time of a Bulgarian peasant

his name begins with G, but he can't pronounce G
so I stop a street-seller and ask the way to a long street

because a woman is arranging flowers
I understand why her hands are thin and her face white.

One late afternoon I look for Dobruja Street in Sophia
with Hussein. He chews his whiskers constantly.

Forest

The forest quickly pulled in its fishing line
and said "Sun". He wrote the sun.

Empty sky. He loved the sky's emptiness.
A cormorant sang. The forest didn't care.

From a valley an old hornbeam laughed,
he thought the wind was passing by.

He left the beeches, shook their branches.
"It's rain" he said. Lightning struck the water.

That's when I knew I was in a forest.
Soldiers were going down the road, double file.

For Homer

I

Homer lived a quiet life. Like mountain roads.
And quietly he prepared—like
water ready to flow—
for the foundations of poetry.

Like all the world's great poets
he studied bird and beast, the ferocious sea,
the days' first flames, the first waves.

This is why Homer alone resembles Homer.

II

We know Homer as the master of long poems
and long suffering.

          So it was on earth
his long cloak and long frame departed and returned.

The Sea Book

I Chaws

I read, stretched out, looked at the sail fish.
All day I kept saying this line to myself.
The weather was cloudy, it's cloudy I said.
I went out, walked around, checked on repairs.
I pulled a long face at the workers. A stone had fallen,
a plank out of place: I put them right. A child
dashed an octopus against pebbles. I smiled at the child
then I went and turned on a closed fountain.
A woman asked for a street and I showed the way.
Suddenly I recalled I was going swimming that evening
so I went to change. I saw day creeping away.
I sat down then and worked at my Sea Book.

II Threewells Street

A whole long day I watched the sea. Great sea.
Storms gathered in. I sat and chiselled out

a skiff. A road lapped its way to the sea,
later going down behind Pazardağ. Barely seen.

A Greek ship off shore was slowing, putting anchor down.
Aganta! I shouted suddenly. The sea echoed back.

The city was water. Water everywhere. Water, water, water.
I threw a fish into the air and the skiff bowed under me.

—The day's shortened, air sharp as a knife! I said.
Then I got up and headed off for Threewells Street.

III   The City

Today I rose early. I woke up the sea.
A man was holding up a squid, showing it off.
I leaned over to look in his eyes, they were sky-blue, round.
He breathed deeply like a heavy labourer.
Three men sat drinking tea and reading the sky.
One was describing the Lodos wind, acting out
the part. "In Bodrum, before Christ, there were only
the Salmakis and Zephyria districts," said another.
I was thinking of the Dorians and Alexander the Great,
of Saint Peter's chateau and the chevalier de Naillac.
At six the sun came up and we all dispersed.

IV   Hay

I was on the coast, I suddenly remembered this today.
I climbed up and looked at the city from a hill.

A ruined monastery remained ruined,
I thought of its monks, a little of their women too.

I bent down and smelled a stem of hay, followed by
the long braying of a donkey, a goat melody. I was enraptured.

A man was painting a rusted boat.
I cast him my "hello" into the boat.

Then off I went to draw a sketch of a chimney.
Looking at myself in the evening light: hay from head to toe.

V Those From Karya

Who are those folk from Karya? Three times I asked. Then
I thought back to yesterday, how I'd been swimming.
I'd seen seaweed. I've wanted to write about it for years
and the sea's depths. Saying this I climbed into bed.
I've a terrible love of my body, my nose, my arms,
my feet; your hairs, my hairs as they rise
on my stomach; my eyelashes and your mouth.
Then my nakedness, my terrible nakedness,
my legs, my groin. That's why I stretch out
my body, why I grow the hairs in my ears.
For my body I say these things. Then? Then
—Who are those Karya folk? I ask, and filmy pipe.

VI Ecology

I'm learning to name plants. Grasses, flowers.
I take up a laurel. This is wormwood I say.

I'm beginning to inspect from several angles
I tear off a wormwood leaf, then its juice

seeps into my hand. I twist off a branch
from its stem. I count the rings

of a long thin willow branch, then place it
in a stream, alert to the world's opulent greens.

So it is, the whole day I stroll around
then suddenly take up the pen to write.

Reading Li Po

In the first dynasty the unit of measure for wheat, cloth, tools, and gold was the sheep:

	40gr. wheat
	20 metres cloth
1 sheep:	2 axes
	3gr. gold

Then gold took the place of wheat, cloth, tools,

                                    the first time round, that is.

And: "The first paper money was seen in China," says Li Po, the greatest of China's poets.

The first shock.

That day, slowly but surely, he left his beard to grow.

Novembers

Have you ever seen a city razed to the ground?
So what if I have? Whenever and where it was

stays with me, my acrid history.

Know this

What is time
a November leaf
a child's vacillating mouth
a rose
a left-over, half-drunk glass of water.

Right over there in Topağacı I have my own rose-seller
his face like a closed shop in November,
like the oldest winds.

Me, I'm like a stopped clock in a far-off station
wind flocks around inside.

Know this.

The History of a Face

I. History

We share with you the same history. The same suns,
the same winds. We pass through the same grape harvest.

The loneliness of a solitary stream
the voices of children playing in a schoolyard.

A morning's rise, its tides, its suddenness;
the endlessness and finality of a rose.

The same rain, the same flood, the same nomadic tribes of wind;
the sameness and indestructibility of dawn.

II. Voice

You are an underground stream
                    in the mountain republic of Burgaz.
I am an ordinary writer
                    in your republic's
abandonment, the one whose job it is to spread
the sparkle of windrows, compasses, soundings and rainbows.

                    So says a voice
deep within our ear,
as if from an old seaman
at the helm of a sunken boat.

When I stopped and looked at you
you were like coppiced trees, like meadows.
Sky swept past
and the eyes of Burgaz seamen were with that passing sky.

As for me, my ears were always pricked to that voice.

III. Exile

You are an island on an ancient map
from which an ancient people take water.

On your island I am the sun, alcohol and boredom.

You are the island's morning, its evening;
I am its night.

You are its waterways, trees, meadows and suns;
I am your nightmare.

You are the people's wheat, their pastures and streams;
I am their desolation.

You are the crowds through which I pass;
I am the exile of your isle.

Inscription on a Grave

"I, Ali Nalbantoğlu, born 1304,
              from Istanköy.
Tallest of three brothers.

Nameless, untitled in this world,
and so too here.

              My legacy?
I crawled my way to seventy-four
And now lay here, in Halikarnassos."

That's an inscription a friend and I
stopped to read at the end of a long lane
one late October
              around noon.

Dead

I

On the Frontier of Pain

The dead write their names in capitals
on the wall of a room pocked with holes.

Casting its shadow full-length
with two letters.

Ears attune to the sound of water
because the blood is fresh

and it will leave its place
for the shore of an uprising.

II

Death

Has death changed its ways or what?
It scares itself

in self-denial.
Its blood.

Its blood seeps out at terrific speed
and gathers.

Now the fire is slowly rising to its feet
because death has been arrested.

III

About to Leave

The dead:
—Who darkened the sky like this?
They say: Ask this
of the poet!

On the frontier of pain
about to leave.

This is one of the questions that will be asked.

IV

Death was scrutinized.

An Old Street in Pera

Birds take to the air above Hagia Irene
stalks of grass behind their ears.

At last you're here I say to myself
here where the roads of an old map meet.

A cat stares at you wide-eyed
and the sky is as low as it gets.

A woman is trying to cross the street. I think of you,
and say the neck I've never seen is terribly thin.

Peddlers, soldiers, knife grinders pass me by
and the sullen faced grave diggers of our world.

A voice says we're with you on the same peninsula,
then vanishes into an old Pera street.

So it is every night I tread an old street in Pera,
every night your mud on my soles.

Poem for a Father Looking for His Lost Son

"How often", he said, "will this boy run away?
He ran away at twelve, at sixteen he's running now."
This is how he spoke, and then fell silent. Pushing
the long hairs of his moustache to the left side of his mouth.
Had he come from Erzurum, or from Tunceli?
For the first time he understood
                              how big the world now was,
then he closed up inside himself
                              watching the bird
hover and circle in the air.

We too fell silent,
                    each locked within ourselves.

What a Woman Sees Each Night from a Coast

Every night she comes alone and sits on the coast.
Every night a large circular saw works away, shrieking.

A bulldozer takes up the road.

Children lorries horses cars
every night that's all she sees.

Apart from that, a desecrated spring, a swallow,
a tree, sometimes too a falling leaf.

And something called the sky
clinging to the corner of her mouth.

An Old Salt

"The weather's turned, it's Lodos behind this," they say.
They set their eyes on the boats at sea.
They read the winds as if from a book
                              of a thousand pages.

"Lodos is a bitch, slippery, my father would say,
and he'd not measure any wind with that,"
said an old sea salt,
                    his face like a wall.

They look as if they haven't heard. As if
their days at sea were spent with cunning Odysseus.
Then, as if taking a sign
                              from the sky's changing form
they rise and go.
          The old salt stays. Eyes pegged to the sea.

View

Unmoving sea. Empty sky. Near oleanders
the old boatman pulls his boat ashore and repairs it.
Bees, and house martins turn above his head.
Not a sound. With his saw, nails and birds
every morning he finds himself part of the scene.
After a while the sea's skin, which we know, moves,
later checkers are pushed in the teahouse.
Then men women and children begin to pass
with water jugs and bundles in their hands.
It's then, at that moment, they stop and wave to him.
Weren't they also part of the scene?

The Man Walking Along a Sunny Coast

Someone is walking along the sunny coast
holding his shadow in his hand, together. Empty
sky.
      In his hands tomatoes peppers cucumbers.
Women passing with their nets. Bees, seaweed,
the sea flat as a plain following on behind.

—They say, winter is around the corner. And quinces
grew early this year. They say, if quinces come early
winter will be long.
        He doesn't hear.
Holds his shadow tightly in his hand,
walks along the coast,
        beyond the wagging tongues.

Visiting the Beloved Wife of a Dead Poet

'Papers, books' she said 'wherever I lay my hand.
A few half-finished poems, another somehow or other
complete. It was all there in the poems, wasn't it?
In one the sky grew pale, in others a street
came and went.
                    That was how we spent our lives.'

Her voice,
        as if coming from far away, faltered,
and then moved on in the quiet room. Then
she showed us a book that lay open on the desk
which the poet had touched, left for the last time.
'He sat there, reading this book,
and then we saw it slip from his hand.
That was all.'

                And that's what she said, her face
behind her hands, as if eclipsed
by the shadow of a passing cloud.

Old Boatmen

Mornings
        they come to the same place and sit.
Stare at the sea. Their voices
as if they were voices from another world.

                —Remember,
the boat was taking water. At the helm
we steered towards death and returned.

—A cormorant,
          crashed down headfirst
into the helm and never came back up.

—That day my funeral flashed before my eyes
passing by
          on the shoulders of friends.

             —Still in my ears
what Ateşoğlu said, We're sinking!

All day they talk like this.
Stubbed out cigarettes between their fingers.
Stare at the sea. Dead sea.
             Sky
comes and goes in the coffeehouse mirror
familiar faces from another time and place.

Evening with a Sprig of Sweet Basil

When she saw a sprig of sweet basil in the door
"Someone called" she said, "whoever could it be?"
She pulled a string, pushed open the door. Looked around.
Three more leaves fell from the vine. Three dry leaves.
She saw the pomegranate splitting, as if for the first time.
She left the onions and salt she carried in the kitchen.
"It's evening" she said, entering the room.
She went to change her clothes, put oil in the lamp.
Put wood in the stove, lit a flame. Noise
coming from her neighbours. Were they frying fish?
Then she sat with evening in her hand,
        that branch of sweet basil.

The Men

The old coffee seller straightens up the stools. The sky
is old. The coffeehouse empty. Olives, chickens, figs.
(On the floor a lime bucket, corn cobs, a water jug.)
        This, just a fragment of the scene.

            Later the men arrived.
Moustaches, full-grown beards. They opened sackcloths.
Ordered tea.
            "Watch out for the pier, I said, that's all!"
One of them said, partly in anger, partly in rage.
"I said the same too" the tallest of them said.
The third, taciturn, listened with his head down.
His face like the front of a darkened door.

            As we watched them talk
each of their moustaches dipped into their tea.
            Then they were suddenly quiet
as if talking about someone who had recently died.
        And before the sun went down they left.

As If Death Were a Daily Routine

The road twists and turns. Eventually we stopped there.
We saw her through the open door,
                        sat spinning wool,
the spindle in her hand.
A large ball of wool had rolled and stopped at the door.
We stretched our heads around the threshold:
                        "How are you?" we asked.
As if changing the place of a chair
"We're dying, see!" She said
                        without raising her head.
As if death were a daily routine.

Wind was pounding the sea in front of her
which now and then she raised her head to see.

A Shoreside Coffeehouse

Day was underway. Had we ordered our sage teas?
Three people sat in a corner patching a net, some
playing dominoes, some of us lighting cigarette
after cigarette. As if the world had stopped,
absorbed in our own and each other's thoughts.
Swallows were striking against the glass outside.
Suddenly a voice, his moustache-rumpled-face
—The sea's gone calm, he said. His eyes,
journeying across the sea, caught us all.
At the end of a long pause
he stood up.
      It was then we saw him
and the calmed sea.
      At that point we came out of ourselves.

Outside the sky was like a slice of bread.

Book of the Dead

I. On the Painful Death of a Discoverer

1.
In the beginning
all day he watched seabirds.

2.
He played dominoes for a year.
Found fault with his friends.

Had his photo taken with night.

3.
His face was a magnet for sun.
(He took only an afternoon snooze.)

4.
For five years in Anatolia's oldest history
he sold herring, salt and milk.
He drank raki, swept shop floors.

Then he discovered Troy.

5.
He died out walking with a panther.
(They say he dyed his beard red.)

II. Conversations on the Life of an Exalted Person, According to Ibn-I Hacer Heytemi

1.
—My father's clothes were neat.
He used excessive scents.
Like Henry IV you could recognise him by his smell before he was seen.

2.
—"His name is remembered with that of a predatory bird."
He chewed frankincense gum to fend off forgetfulness.

3.
—We stayed with him for one year.
He never once took a rest.

4.
—He never sat in the shade of his creditor's trees.
Words dissolved like candy in his mouth.

5.
—Summers he worked in the silk trade.
He gave all of his profit away.

I swear not one of his race were slaves.

6.
—He never had a concubine
And cried before he prayed.

7.
—One day he saw a soldier eating meat
And asked how long the fish had lived.

I Woke Saying I Love You Three Times

I woke saying I love you three times
I got up and changed the water in the vase
I saw a cloud had just upped sticks and left.

Your face was fallen as if from some part of the morning.

I kicked out a poem with half-finished streets and balconies
Got bored, made food, dried myself some herbs
My cherry laurel! I heard a voice say.

Your face was like the first days of the Republic.

I went out and walked around up and down
I read some poems and formed an affinity
I felt your clove-gum smelling breath on me.

I wear you out remembering but still you're beautiful.

Poet and Voices

Every day he comes and takes his place in the world.
"The difficult thing," he says "is to live the life of poetry,
writing always comes later." The words come easy
from his mouth, like ordering a glass of water.
Then, to be more at home with himself
he goes as usual to his old chair and sits.
Comes face to face with trees, with seas and skies.
He twirls a carnation in his hands. Brings it to his nose.
Then listens to the voices. To someone saying goodnight,
someone passing in the street. Mornings' noisy departure.
Silent grass. Descending day.
                           Voices. Voices. Voices.
All day he listens to these sounds
and then withdraws
                 to his place in the world.

Hamam Street

Returning, sunlight filled the street,
sunlight on your face.
            The road,
was it twisting? We saw the women.
Sky, as if it were their embroidery,
with flocks of birds they'd brought down,
                        ashen.

They went to put oil in the lamps, then
gathered up their needlework, their birds,
            from the life of the street.

We were sick with love,
            do you remember?
From behind us a flock of swallows took flight.

The Women

They stop by the harbour wall and are talking.
Their voices stir birds into flight; leaves are falling.
Who knows to which age these women belong.

You know, it's as if sometimes the world stops,
one day we were together pressing flowers
into a notebook:
                    they're like that, women,
who knows when, or where, all at once
a voice from our past
                    is right beside us.

In the Sea's Wake

We were walking. Were we walking? Sun went down.
You beat around like sea against the coast.

A boy
barged past, in the corner of his mouth
a stem of grass.

That faded day in 1979
your mouth was two green leaves
and I was there in your mouth's rose.

(A woman on the Council Estate
opened and closed her windows,
readied, with time for evening.)

from The Secret History of Poetry

*"In the Tang dynasty civil servants were chosen
for their knowledge of poetry."*

Poets are island dwellers…

*

All poets are in the service of masters. Just as all shoeshines work for the best…

*

The difficult thing is to live the life of poetry; writing always comes later.

*

Poetry is a foetus.

*

It's an image thing. With the poet it comes into existence. That's why every poet has their own way of using image, an image-key: a key that allows him to open and close the lock of his own devising.

*

If a poem is written and goes out into the world, something in the world has changed.

*

Poetry is contrary to all forms of correctness, even itself.

*

Poetry is spontaneous. A sea, a tree, a face, a street that's suddenly there.

*

Poetry is wild. It's where the kick comes from.

*

Poetry is a hidden spring. It cannot be opened or explained; the thing it wants to explain, to show, is itself.

*

It's the job of poetry to light fires.

*

Poets are children. I don't mean they don't grow up. They do, but always as children grow. The oldest they reach is adolescence.

*

The language of poetry is a language used nowhere else.

*

Poetry is on paper.

Mostly it's a single page. That's where it gives colour, where it's born and lives...

That's why, as soon as the poem begins to take form in the poet's mind, he sees the page.

*

Poetry is interrogation.

*

Residues:

1.
The coffin was opened and the waking face seen.

2.
Her voice was like the flight of a child's kite.

3.
The long wishing-thread was never broken.

4.
Time came when the horse became its own saddle.

*

To whoever and whenever poems come they pull you to one side. From that point on the sky is no longer the sky.

*

Poets carry people, cities, rivers and streets in their pockets.

*

The poet destroys to rebuild...

*

What poetry writes is silence. A silence like the stopping of the world, the severing of its breath.

*

Faultless, perfect poems are not easy to write. But the truly difficult thing is to write easy, flawed poems.

*

Shelley was infatuated with the image-power of Bacon's essays. He looked at them with the eyes of a poet. It needn't surprise us. For the same reason I too look at a lot of prose with a poet's eye. And a lot of poems from the point of view of prose.

The sole key that opens and closes the poem is image.

*

Poets write in parentheses…

1984-1996

from **Delta And Child**

Passer-By

A swift, a puddle, a piece of sky.
They must have dropped from a poem.

So said the passer-by.

Sage

They left with sage in their mouths.
In those days man had the power to create silence.

Clocks

That day he left home, sat beside the sea,
and the shade read ten degrees late on the sundial.

Quinces

—Eat quinces!
God will even take note of that.

Autumn

March enters the plain, so it's autumn in the mountains!

Birds

Empty sky. Birds fly in from the right.

Forest

Somewhere, someplace, a forest has entered a poem.

Tobacco

When I wrote all this I was fifty-one
and my quilts smelled of tobacco.

Black Amber

One should start with your mouth when describing you.
My child, your mouth is Chinese silk, fires, black amber

Your mouth is a cold-water spring, a general strike
A foolish sea throwing itself from place to place

Your mouth is the boy selling dark blue birds in the market
It's a three-monthly magazine called *Field*

Our small rivers are your mouth
Coming down a narrow street each day into a small square

Your mouth is time in Bursa, covered bazaars
The night written in ancient letters

Your mouth is children, birds and summer days
Your mouth is the feel of silk in my mind.

Now As a Little Rose Goes Through the World

Wet your hair like that and ask night to comb it
Now as a little rose goes through the world
Let it tell of a shore-pounding death
Death which comes now, and then later
Death that dries wild flowers in notebooks
Death as a pale, silent easterner
Death that is a mountain or a river
Death that talks to itself as if talking to you
Death like death itself

Yes, wet your hair like that and ask night to comb it.

Each Day I Walk from One End
of a Market to the Other

It's my death, the thing you stand before
Its memory a washed out shore
Perhaps a tree-lined lane we once passed
(In the form of evening
                    a time of love-making)
For tree-lined lanes do have a soul,
Whatever
        that is.

You are a rose,
                oh rose!
(So much, much more, so very much)
Each day I walk from one end of a market to the other
Looking at trees, pausing by a fountain
A bird draws up the whole street with its flight
- A little later your face
I think to myself
A woman's baroque laundry hangs on a line
Pours its brilliant white breath into my mouth
Later, you hold me delicately, kiss me
Once more I walk from one end of the market to the other.

Thank You

Yes, it was for your mouth, always open, moving;
For this, the fractious blue of the sky;
For the apple scented Turkish you spoke
For this miserable, worthless memory of death
For the streets that everyday become a marketplace
For your voice like children returning from school

For all this, for all of these, I thank you.

Beautiful River

My little love, this is your voice, beautiful river
One kissed first by the wind and then by me
These unfinished poems are your ankles
Your breath, your scent, your belly, your shaded eyes
Your bare breasts, your full lips
Your large eyes like this till morning
Your slender form, your hair, your red mouth
Then this bed on which we made love
Then this, my time-worn old face
Your pubis, your filly neck, your infant hands
I look you up and down this way
Entangling our incredible hands and feet.

Yesterday I Wasn't at Home, I Took to the Hills

The sun fathers a cloud in my pocket. I wrote: the stone is blind. Death has no future. Things have only names. And: "A name is a home." (Who was it said that?) Yesterday I wasn't at home, I took to the hills. A gorge looked at us, what it said still lingers in my mind. It was this: we sensed infinity within it. Objects are held in time. The tailors' lamplighter Hermusul Heramise's goatskin rose to its feet every spring. Rain cannot not rain. Stone, not fall.

What was I saying, the world has no thoughts. Grasses don't get bored. A pencil thinks it is a tree. The horizon, a hoopoe. I don't know about you, the world is here to be mythologized. It has, therefore, no other end. Transforming into a myth, to be a myth! That's what we call eternity.

Wherever I start, that's where I return. So I'm going. I have work to do on that grand statement, death.

There Have Been Trees I Have Made Friends With

"I filled silence with names." Codified things. I have known the sky's and the trees' infancy. There have been trees I have made friends with. There still are. I didn't understand the Milky Way. Nor numbers. (They behaved as if they had yet to be discovered.) Except for eight (5+3) with whom I became intimate friends. (Who hasn't?) A little with zero too. (It's not been so easy to find zero.) I've heard terrible things about three. Why? I don't know. To know is a number. And I've also met one. You can't think with one. Some numbers are born guilty. One of them is one. I loved stones without asking why. The relation between the pebble's name and its shape has not been proved. I couldn't find a thing on the history of black amber. Fine. Mystery is everything. There are some consonants I couldn't read. (The letter's spirit abounds in consonants. American Indians knew this well.) I accompanied birds. Except for the turtledove, birds know nothing of numbers. Horses, I understood, don't dream in the East. (In Homer horses weep.) I have seen mountains while walking. And thinking as they walked. Recognition impedes reason. *The World is ours!* Said the snails, talking among themselves. I can't say I understand that. Nor that I don't understand it. One should read snails.

As you talk about rivers the rivers themselves are talking, grasses are in their eyes. Time is an illusion. Write this down somewhere. It's not true that spirit has no outward facing view. Jesus' ghost still roams the earth. (I only ask. It's only to question that one writes.) Those who forget their youth stagger in the morning. The rose exists because it is named. Stone got its name when its face was found. (Which is why masons turn stones around and around in their hands.)

I want to return to your eyes. And then... There's no such thing as "then." "Then" is outside history.

Letters and Sounds

Shihabüddin Fazullah spoke with thirty two letters and did not have a soul. He believed in letters and earned a living knitting skull caps. It is said he saw every letter in the human face. In the Zeyl he wrote to Cavidan (which hasn't been found), he assigned the letter A to sky; to water: C (water is from Thales); to death: U (Death is a bit U). To fire: Z.

The world was the letter, all forms. Sophocles, who like Pythagoras, did not know how to draw, was also of the letter, as was the cricket, and Mohammed too.

Mohammed (whom we know spoke with twenty eight letters and had a soul and no bird could ever have flown to where he did) gave ear to sounds. He listened only to them. Everything was sound. Heaven and Hell were sound. A peacock was sound. If Tu Fu rode to Rice Pudding Mountain to graze his horse, it was sound. Which is why he always felt a void between the soul and the forms. And why he seldom wrote. Why should he? Language is lonely. It doesn't speak. The universe is more talkative than us, he said. More leaf-filled. The sun speaks with images. A tree works noisily. So does a stone. Night descends in noise. The universe is sound.

"The alphabet is a peddler."

Whichever Angle We Take, Everything Explains Itself

Everything, everything began in the moon-watching city of Babel.

Names followed. Once named, everything became boring. The silence was broken. The enormous silence.

In history there are no animal names to be found, you say*. Nor the sounds of flowers' names… yet sound… is everywhere.

I don't forget that everything had its place in the world. I saw that Time became unrecognizable once it acquired a name. A bird couldn't remember its name any-old-how. As for the mountains, not one of them knew its name.

Wonderful.

To name something is death!

Whichever angle we take, everything explains itself.

Mehmet the Conqueror was short.

Amos was a farmer of Pharaoh figs.

Al Farabi was swarthy.

If only we'd never known names. The world we see through names is not the world. That's why we go to our graves never having seen the earth. There's nothing without its own weight. We should have started from here. Mad Time was left outside. We were separated. Now whatever we write we write about death; death and time.

I don't know why but these days I read death vertically. Try it yourself. It's worth it.

I'm cutting it here. I hear a blade of grass talking as it does. I'll also be at the bird's birthday party. Night awaits me. We know the way.

* History, this phallus memory.

120

I Don't Want to Think

Nothing's as old as this world. The sky is sick. The sun is ordinary. The trees are unskilled. Every morning a Bedu goes to work on his camel. Every evening two Chinese walk their bird.

The world is a repetition. A tree looks a thousand years into the future. Sees a dinosaur a thousand years away. Ghazali used to liken himself to the number 7. Homer used to walk every morning.

There is nothing new to the eye.

This is terrifying.

Was it Goethe who said "Time is my field"? I don't want to know. From where it sits a house overlooks Montevideo. The chair is urban. The window is feudal. Water ran without memory. The soul is alone. When I was a child I wanted to be a river. Rivers always called to me. I don't want to think. The world thinks for me instead.

The word is dead.

Bronze: Monarchic.

Iron: Democratic.

One evening I suddenly saw that the world had grown old. Seeing wore me out.

Askelopis

Askelopis used to walk around with a bird from Ephesus and could see what we couldn't. Objects are like that; not everyone can see them. They love secrecy. Like poets, they too speak in a white language. Reason cannot grasp it. Yet there is nothing that is invisible. Objects don't know this. Why should they? After all, it's not for objects to know. Do fish know the water in which they swim? I recognized the forest without knowing it, and never forgot it*. There's no way of stopping them, once objects turn into words. They envelope the world, then turn into thousands of sentences. In some corner of the world, every morning, a thousand objects wake for this. I came to know the world through sentences. The outer limits of the universe. Language is the only god, that foetus!

(My beloved language, do not conceal those untrodden paths and keep me from seeing them.)

There's nothing more to objects than this. This much Askelopis could not see. Death revealed this to him.

(Doesn't philosophy, after all, teach us something about death?)

Would you say objects are lonely?

From now on objects will never feel this kind of loneliness again.

I promise.

* O memory, there's no escaping you!

Rocks

Rocks I

They're talking   about rocks
      I was a rock

         I heard them

Rocks II

I grew

       in rock
       reach out

         to me

Rocks III

A rock

       and a hill
are talking about death

     watching water

Rocks IV

Hey

    rocks

        I'm evenings'
         spirit

Towards Evening

I undressed   your voice
                    said
towards evening your voice is sky

Fern

My name   is fern
          in the mouths
                    of rivers

Garden

Strolling in the garden
grass apparently

          saw

               you

Death Is Like Nothing Else

A waterlily leaf
swims
on the water's face:

Death is like nothing else.

Leaf

Leaf

doesn't know its shade
until

it falls to you.

Shadow Falls Across the Courtyard

Between the marshmallows
a tortoise
sticks out its head to see:

its shadow falls across the courtyard.

Stopping

You stopped

silence
stripped
you.

Goat Track

I'm a goat track
winding to you

just as
e
v
e
n
i
n
g

a
p
p
r
o
a
c
h
e
s

As I Write

As I write
the paper
hears

you.

Ashes and End

Farewell
sky
fare-

well.

What the Tree Says

Leave me alone
says a tree
okay okay

I'll talk.

Trees

Trees
ask,
brothers

who exactly are we?

Words II

You suppose

they tell of rivers
when words

talk of you.

Blonde-Haired Child

An open gas tap inscribes your name

I look you over with my mouth
I find you stuffed into oversized telephone books
I descend to your postage-stamp eyes
How a leaf
Noisily
Falls

That's how

I love you
Blonde haired child.

1997-2008

from Things That Count Things That Don't

Lyre

Thor was getting carried away with the rock's lyre.
René Char

1.

To write every poem by demolishing the ones before…
This is writing.

2.

And I've always wanted to try that Chaos, where reality reaches its
furthest limits in language, where that relationship between language and
reality's other side comes to a halt, and how it comes to a halt. Maybe this
was just a curiosity. But I tried it. Because I know there can be no talk of
poetry if meaning (and reality) isn't overcome.

How is it to live in Chaos, to write of it? This curiosity never left me.
To live with the loss of the subject's sovereignty, changing place with the
object (even for a short time…)

To set out on such a journey… To draw near to the subject from all
sides; but never fully grasp it: only *to circle it*. To start going round again
just when you draw near…

3.

Meaning is seldom grasped in a good poem.
But it always seems that you've grasped it.
It doesn't take refuge only in a certain meaning.
It forms mountain chains like the words of prophets.

4.

Only poets can never be outside language, no matter how.
Only language makes hope a reality.

5.

Emerson talks of the '*fossil poems*' of the language.
It ought to be called the untouched language.
The poem's horizon starts there.

6.

Objects, like images, are given to poets.
But objects spread fear!
I always felt this.

7.

The poem is where the word disappears, the place where it is almost
impossible to fix meaning.
A place, as if not a place.
Because here language stops speaking.
It says nothing.
Sensing, only.

8.

To write language involves only that:
Essence is all it needs.

'*With the inner voice*' (Maurice Blanchot).

9.

When I finish a poem I view it as if it were not mine.
Much later I know it's mine.

(The sun wants to know where it sinks.)

10.

Every poem harbours death, violence (violence and writing, one
inside the other), darkness.

(I read that bees collect pollen from among empty flowers.)

11.

I'm always suspicious of poems I understand.
I look at the world as images, I see it that way.
(Like children.)
Images are my home.

12.

I could say that it was almost always my aim to rout (*sous rature*)
the poem.

13.

The lyre and the poem are strangers to each other.
 (A distant poem, line of the horizon…)

14.

Only poets have no hope.

Stones

...And I will give him white stone
and on that stone will be written a name
unknown to all except the receiver.
GOSPEL OF JOHN

I

Listen to stones,
to what they say,

        most of all.

II

Instantly
stones begin to talk to us,

but they do not know us.

III

Stone
calls stone:

(There is only the named.)

IV

Lean over, look
at the stone;
with both eyes.

Maybe you see a face.

V

Time,

      is time

on stone.

VI

Stones should be touched.
An ethic ought to arise,

from touching.

VII

You should learn
to read stones.

To walk
with them too.

VIII

Does amber
have hands?

Here's a question.

IX

It's doubtful
whether words
can express stones.

I don't know if words know this.

X

Has a paving stone
ever laughed?

— No one knows.

XI

Night,
sleeps in stone.
That's why I carved

you out of stone.

XII

Listen, to stones.
It's voice, of silence.

XIII

Word,
falls upon stone.

Stones,
will always take time.

Golden Oriole

If it's necessary to liken him to the Middle Ages, then he's like one of those medieval travellers with sceptre, sack cloth and a humble face.

Like the prophets he studied the magical language in caves, made friends with Sufis, alchemists, Kabbalists, to foretell the future; he interpreted the Bible according to Iblis; he thought of it as profit, those things poetry had dug from death (poets and death are neighbours), the last traveller.

(You know what I mean.)

Enis Batur.

A poet.

We could also say a petal.

A golden oriole.

A protruding sea.

A monk.

A prophet too.

(Why do I say that?

I don't know either why I say that.)

Maybe the road isn't one we know, it's the one we take.

That's why.

Anyway the road takes its name in the end.

An end that is silence.

Finally he girds himself with silence, hopelessness,

The end, and leaves.

That's what fell to him.

What is it that we call the world?
With its people, trees, birds, slugs.
A book.
Of a thousand pages.[3*]
He has been working on this book.
He has taken hopelessness and ordinariness on his croup.
(Hopelessness was there right from the beginning, never will it leave.)
This time he'll find out about ordinariness.
And he knows something else: Poets have no life!
In fact aren't people, animals, a puddle of water, a handful of grass, and insects waiting in single file in the two mouths of the road just to get a place in this book?
But he covets the road.
He sees it.
He's taking it over.

[3*] For everyone, voluminous, polyphonic: double meanings, remote associations, exits, open-door metaphors, dashes, parentheses, margins, cut ups, full stops, independent images, blanks, collages, a book with internal-external texts: Sun, eclipses, winds, tides, acid nights, radio nights, loneliness, happiness, unhappiness, propane gas, alcohol, and death…

Table

I

Of all things (in the silent world)[4*] perhaps only the table is the clearest, the simplest. Openness, clarity, is the table's basic principle: It resembles nothing other than itself. And reveals itself with its very first breath. And as a word it doesn't contradict its image: It's that, whatever it is: It's never ambiguous. And not only this: it's solid, simple. Its solidity can say nothing other than table. Clarity shines from all four sides of the table. And it throws its entire existence into this: It lives by embracing its name.[5†] Perhaps it's through its name that it comes to understand its existence. In fact everything should start this way.

[4*] The silent world immediately calls out for a bracket. It questions everything: According-ing to who?

[5†] A name-giver. But it doesn't see the name as an unrealized chorus of voices. It behaves like a fundamentalist. A fundamental cynic: He must be saying the opposite of 'I see the horse very well but not the horsemanship.' He says he who sees the horse also sees the horsemanship.

This way we should hold an endless examination of the world of things; we should grasp what is there at our fingertips. Like this we can raise the curtain of another world. Everything has an inner and an outer world: The existence of objects rests in this difference: Existence contains many meanings. It's how it protects its weight. (Suddenly I understand the weight set by the souls of things!) Whereas the table's inner world is set out like this, its outer world is clear too. It can be seen from everywhere. It's not surprising. The table is mostly table from the outside. It's more realistic that way. More itself.[6*]

In
brief.

[6*] We might say a secret liberalist. Its necessity is singular: Happiness. An urgency from birth. Quiet, inward looking. A bit slovenly, insensitive (hair a little long). It places everything before it and lives: without knowledge of secrecy.

II

Table is a privilege: Simple. Brave. Solid. (Simple, because it has no other pieces.) It's not clear why it feels this is necessary. Things also have a life, in their opinion. The table puts this down right at the beginning. Wanted it to be known this way. (Besides, where isn't there privilege?) Maybe this is why it's a fundamentalist. And for this reason also a moralist. (It's in the nature of table to need morals.) Becoming more of a commander. Is it possible that it wanted this? Well yes, and no. But at least it's possible it thought about it. That's certain. Because every table is a personality. It's not easy to say that it likes everywhere. But again, this is a fact: Let's not take up the table and put it just anywhere, for once we put a table somewhere it invades the place immediately. In an instant it's part of that place.[7*]

[7*] When, in a house, you find a place for everything large or small, when you come to the table you stop: Where should the table be put? The table always makes us ask such questions. And it doesn't end there: What will we do with the chair? You see, one more question.

An ordered man likes order. So everything in a room is ordered according to him. An egoist.[8*] This needs to be understood. In truth he's a pluralist. Of course, in his opinion. (What isn't opinion?). Once a dinner table, it becomes an activist, its pluralist vein swells at once. It says: *Let no one be left standing!* If it's a writing table, you can't get all that near to it. You can't get close because it's introverted: It lives listening to itself. It talks to itself too. (In a language unlocked only by Kabbalists.)[9†]

The table always takes a duty upon itself. An office table has no individual freedom: it's everyone's. The table knows this. It opens its arms immediately and embraces it. The table we're talking about is a little like this. It's for this it works. It's on the table things come together. And can only be thought of and decided on the table. The table is the basis for everything. There is no escape from tables.

[8*] A commander. Strict. Uncompromising. Can we also say a wise spirit? Silent. Calm. Good.

[9†] Its journey is similar to the journey we made under the shadow of death: No more, no less: Sensation deficit: Don't look for meaning! Use it. *Lord of the body, looking down.*

III

What is the nature of table?
Bertrand Russell asks.
Openly, clearly.
Then (as the thing found opposite us):
Four-legged, a rectangle with four wide angles facing each other.
Measured.
Balanced.
Stable.
Stable because it's born that way.
Wooden or metal.
Horizontal.
Horizontal because that's how it will exist.
Solid.
Solid because it's a whole.
It has a form, a depth, a weight.
And like all things it's 'a thing'.
(You know things, they live alone. They don't let anyone interfere
with their business.)
And again like all things it has a history.
Harmonious.
Sedate.[10*]

[10*] And perhaps only the table can talk of dignity. So why did we say a moralist?

Table fills the place it's in with magnificence.
　　You should see it then.
　　But the table's beauty isn't seen straight away.
　　We are content with its presence.
　　And this is enough for us.[11*]
　　Usually we forget about it.[12†]
　　We understand table when we stand over it.
　　Then we talk with it.
　　When a book falls from the table:
　　We both bend down and pick it up together.
　　We say 'a book fell'.
　　(Both of us together.)
　　And the table works concealed inside (like us)
　　And weaves silence like us.
　　Exalted silence!
　　It daydreams in fact.
　　Tables always do that.
　　(Its existence requires it.)

[11*] Actually our interest in objects is nothing more than us wanting to be known, to be understood by them.

[12†] Of course the table couldn't care less. Why should it? And maybe tables talk about this forgetting amongst themselves. It's unknown. They say things have no knowledge of sense. In fact everything is alive. This is always overlooked. On the other hand, things don't always use it. And reality doesn't always need to be transparent.

IV

I have an abnormal life with my writing materials as with all other
materials. It's endless. And moreover with my table, and almost
everything on my table, I talk. Every time I leave the room I say
"goodbye". I never once look upon them as mere "space fillers". What
is the world anyway but for these things? Every moment, everywhere,
we live under the weight of this world of things. Everywhere objects call
out to us. This call is something big.
This is why above all else I love my table.
And so it is but for all the love I rain down on my table
I'm still afraid to ask if it's pleased with me or not.
Because there's nothing it hasn't suffered at my expense.
It seems to me that I can only ever show my true self, my difficulties,
my foul temper, my rudeness, my shabbiness,
my instability to it alone.
You see that's why I can't ask.

The Moral

I always had big, long tables, I always worked at big, long tables.
I loaded all of my things on it too. First the dictionaries,
then the real writing materials: Pencil, felt pen, cartridge pens:
Skrips, Parkers, especially Pilot Hi V5, extra fine;
Faber Castell, calligraphy pen 2.0; 20, 30, 50 Rapidos
(you have to hold your hand upright to write, to draw with them,
there's no other way); different kinds of nibs, big small,
especially nibs for hatching (and they are the most beautiful of all
and they draw beautiful lines); different sizes and colours of ink (Pelikan),
files (that are always sparking with dreams); pencils that I've gathered from
all over the world, (that never once lose their way); largely Johann Faber, 2200;
Fatih 4B, Schwann; erasers (there's none better than Technics Pro 20s); big
and small
scissors, primarily with stainless steel blades; or unknown (since everything is
for cutting);
gouache, oils and water colours; different sized brushes; knives, a pocketknife;
(one branded *Ilhan of Bursa* always right next to me); Top-Exes,
a lot of Toners (that don't dry or spill easily); cut and left, coloured writing
papers
with or without writing on; two nail files size big and small;
a Sony hand radio; a huge, white and blue, beaded plate
(for drying fruit); a Baby Hermes typewriter (we're almost the same
age); thick, thin javelin pens; razors, rotrings blue azure,
deep red, weiss white, brown maroon; glues, staplers, post-it notes 3m.;
rulers (pioneering the line), pins, drawing pins,
book marks etc... And what about my pipes, my tobaccos (once upon a time
I had my hands on them all the time, but these days maybe once or twice
I rarely hold them now), aren't they still part of the table's inventory,
and only the table's? Doesn't it hold the writing's hand, who could say
the opposite? On the other hand, because I work at three different places,
on three tables, if not all, then can't most of them be replicated?

Roundness

Do you know roundness?

Who doesn't?

Where doesn't the eye see it, distinguish it, and is then arrested by it?

Locked inside the world of things, immanent. What could be more natural for an object? It will retreat far into itself and look out from there. It will keep all that it sees to itself, share it with no one, burying in its closed world as with all others of its kind.

Is it destiny?

Destiny too is something like this. Because it chose itself, it expects nothing at all from the world. And of all things what could be more introverted than the circle

itself?

A concealed realist.

Esoteric.

On its door hangs a huge sign saying: No Entry!

Like a circle it starts from one point and again comes back to it, placing itself in a hoop.

An Aristotelian.

That's the way it is, but we can't really say that roundness excludes the external world: Because life is round. Still, if there's something it does exclude, it's geometry. The circle rejects geometry's domain. (It does its best not even to recall its name.) It embraces everything. Without ever changing. Don't we see its various outward forms everywhere? What else could assume a thousand and one forms like this?

There's nowhere its imperialism doesn't extend, as it wraps itself around iron, stone, wood, glass and soil: Forever taking its place next to us in the form of a plate, a spoon, a vase, a clock, a chair, a mirror, a glass, a lamp, a cupboard, a table, a globe, a ball etc… A chameleon! It appears too in everything we eat and drink. Eggs, onions, garlic, potatoes, cauliflowers (dear cauliflower), celery, cabbage, turnips, melons, grapes, watermelons.

There's nowhere it doesn't place or stretch a hand or leg. It's a townsman, mainly. A captain of industry. Its influence continues everywhere. It turns its back on geometry too and laughs.

It turned the world upside down by turning into a wheel.

And so inscribed speed on earth (how should speed be explained, this contemporary dynamo?). And only speed? Didn't it also teach us silence (silence is a revolution too)?

And roundness itself is its content. (Geometricians have never yet perceived the true essence of roundness, limiting themselves to its outer edge. They never really thought of its inner space as something full, beyond the limits of reason. They recognize the world as something flat, empty. As if its essence had been discarded. As if they had said understanding isn't our job. It's doubtful they even know we live inextricably with roundness.) Roundness is an atlas of meaning. It can be seen from all sides, it is beyond our imagination.

Difficult to read like an atlas too. And if we follow Jaspers: Every presence conceives of itself as round. The natural state of roundness is necessarily internal, not external. (It is unique to us to experience the surface superficiality in everything.) What is it that's empty inside? Emptiness also has a language, a meaning, like fullness. Like all of us it's conscious of it too. As a shape on earth (such as roundness), no other shape can convey the sense of touch, the play of our hands on it. Whatever shape it assumes, it becomes life itself. Closed, yes, tight-lipped but its nature requires it. Secretive too. It has to think and solve everything on its own. It closes its windows and lives like that. (Place all the round, secretive objects there are in the world before your eyes, and think!) No one can complete with roundness: it assumes forty appearances: it makes no concessions, but it's no bigot. It knows how to break out of its shell when necessary. By breaking into a thousand pieces (of course whoever did escape with their identity intact?) it adopts and takes on a thousand different shapes. As if giving the first examples of the art of puzzle-making. But not like a Gestalt theorist, entering into the order, the nature of its own world, following its own mark: but as the handle of a cup, the decorative frame of a window, a clock's allure, everything on a surface (as a full-stop, a footnote in a piece of writing)…

Despite its allure we can't really say it's been liked. But like some people: we can't rigidly say "An object should know how to be loved, and if it doesn't, then that's its problem." I, for one, can't do it.

Roundness, as a word, never stirred the curiosity of poets. It starts with R and ends in S. As if for poets it incurs no meaning. Two celled. Nor is it a word you can articulate in a single breath. For the O (one of the vowels of roundness) you need to stick out the lips, like this:

ROUNDNESS.

Are we therefore going to shake it and throw it around? Besides, everything requires a bit of effort; roundness too (as a word) has a right to ask this. Anyway, it's not true that roundness has some kind of deficit of meaning:

a) in the language of philosophy it's a symbolist
b) special to psychology
c) a rationalist in geography
d) an intellectual in history (we could say the first Kantian)
In point of fact it's the foundation of the most beautiful sentences:
THE WORLD IS ROUND!

And isn't it, when all is said and done, the halo of our love? Who could not, with all its sincerity, feel it close to them?

Slug

I

From out-
side it looks as if it inscribes a circle but when time comes to close
back in from whence it came suddenly it retracts both ends of the line
and darts inside.

A bungalow.

Spherical.

Shape of shapes.

You see it resembles nothing other than itself.

But if we must compare it to something, then let's say a restless water
drop.

(Armoured, solid, luminous)

In a shell as thin as a membrane and so strong, transparent

A spiral

Alluring.[13*]

When you touch its shell with your forefinger:

—Ping!

you'll hear a sound. Or

— Crack!

when it's broken.

When you take it and look at it in your hand you'll see it creates a
spiral bandage which wraps its beautiful shell like a ball.

(Fast growing and discarded.)

But still, think of it as a dark well.

Or a bottomless well.

One you can descend into but never get out.

Or we could call it a clever puzzle.

(Existence is dialectical.)

[13*] Didn't William Blake call you 'holy'?

(Whenever I, the weak, try to draw that sphere hasn't it always stumbled and fell?)

Didn't it get that shape anyhow after a long and arduous journey?

For this introverted curved line (crookedness props up the world) didn't it wrangle with geometry?

A small world.

Solid.

Dark.

II

From in-

side, then we'll start from the shell's mouth, from that intractable place. From that place, according to botanists, where it beds down for its winter sleep, from where it turns and twists its form from top to midriff.

Isn't everything there?

Lungs (they almost take up all the space), heart (which is a slug itself), bogey-rag (it being the bogey-bug, we know it owes its existence to it, or at least to its clumsiness, slugs are clumsy), intestines (stretching from one end to another), vagina (always at the ready), anus (sensual), brain (with its cover not opened yet), tongue (that comes and goes), tentacles (always at the ready, and isn't that where its eyes are?) etc.

It will look from there at this place we call the world: Retracting its antennae, purveying every inch of the ground it passes, with one foot slowly (slowly? In one minute it can cover 1.12m—1.85m) it will raise its home on its back and traverse a continent.

(I wonder if it's doing exactly that while I'm writing this?)
Then let's leave it, let it crawl on through!

Offering

Tell me, slug, do you love me?

Dear slug, you are one of my many loved, despised, strange, pitiful residents; for how long I have wanted to write about you, how often the pen came to my hand only to fall from it, the paper sliding away—today is destiny. When I started this I believed I would write about you better than all the other insects. (Perhaps it's because we've known each other for so long or because of the special love I have for you [special, yes, but I still haven't fathomed it].) I carried this consuming wish within; you can't imagine how overjoyed I am that I can do this now. Overjoyed because like all the many creatures that come into my little house and follow me from place to place, on my pens and papers, you're one of my friends; and now you appear among my commonplace writings.

How could I not be overjoyed?

Farewell.

Bra

A magical, sensual jewellery box in the history of things:
the bra.[14*]

If you ask its neighbouring words like brace, bracelet, or bracken
(o beautiful rustling bracken) they'll call it ordinary, unimportant, a
meaningless word.[15†] Yet few words are as enticing, sexual, alluring.

It goes far beyond the object it names, it posits only its own being,
presses it forward, emphasizes.[16‡]

It uses only provocative, sexual pathways and labyrinths.

It thrusts out from there.[17§]

---

14 * Why shouldn't we call it the innocent Eros?
15 † Words breed meaninglessness. And they use that meaningless as they see fit.
16 ‡ Isn't it breathless and consumed with the fire of its own kibla?
17 § It craves abandon in moments of dizzying ecstasy.

As if it sought intoxication, wanting to live and die intoxicated.
Happy like that.
And why not?
Besides, the object of happiness is darkness.[18]
It lives with the great dream of the body.[19]

---

18 * It defies description. Is unknown. Incomprehensible.
19 † It grew up in caves, came and went with orgasms and little deaths.

Mud

I

Mud, a name.
And like all that have names it has a history.
From a silent world.
(The silent world is our real world.)
And like all objects, an object.
Yet it has no definite form.
It sleeps on the floor.

It only has a face.
The face of mud, its only form.

Like all other worldly things it lives by retreating into itself.
From the earth's surface, yes.
A gru.
It's there with the earth:
The way it thinks of itself on the earth, that's how it finds itself.

It's as if it was never ashamed to be mud.
To be was enough perhaps.
It just wanted a place, like everything else.
It was overjoyed to find itself the soil on a road.
It expected nothing more than a simple life.
And it got it.

II

Everything looks a little like something else, but mud resembles nothing.

Everything can be compared with something else, but mud can't be compared with anything.

Everything in this world has a use, but mud is useless.

Everyone has someone in the world, but mud has no one.

III

Mud is unlovable.
And why?
Nobody knows.
Maybe because of its name.
(It starts off slandering until it's up to its neck in filthy jobs.)
Ok but, what's this to mud?
It's not that simple just to call mud, mud.
It has a place in the world, like all of us.
And like us too it has a name.
Is it such a small thing to have a name?
Knowing this alone ought to be enough for us.
Everything has a certain immunity.
But not mud.
Wherever we see it, we step over it.
Its very existence is almost unbearable for us.
And yet, like other common things, mud is mysterious.

Offering

Look, have a good hard look at mud: You'll love it! Everything has a
         personality.
I lived with things that do not count as much as others that do.
By entering into the writing of someone like me, mud enlarged me.

    O passers-by!
    Be sparing, don't hurt the mud.

Sparrow

Of all the names perhaps the names of birds, streets, and trees are the
        most beautiful.[20]*
Especially bird names.
Counting only those that begin with 'a' would be enough.
Beginning with Albatross, Anhinga, Ash-throated Crake.
But there are none better than those starting with 's':
Swift, Snipe, Saffron Finch, Sanderling, Spotted Sandpiper
And especially the quickest to say: Sparrow.[21]†
Which bird is as tender, as beautiful?
But the sparrow's real beauty comes from its modesty, from its ordinariness.
And ordinariness is its true self.[22]‡
It passes its time with thrown-off things and yet it does not sacrifice its
        pleasure (yes, its pleasure) for anything.[23]§

---

20 * Names are voices. We know them by sounds. Letters are the shadows of names.
People can't do without names, and will name no matter what.
21 † Who doesn't know the sparrow? Two syllables but as if they were one. Who first gave
the sparrow its name, I don't know. But I'd like to know what the sparrow thinks of it.
22 ‡ Is it easy to be ordinary? And not only that: which bird is content with its name, its
reputation?
23 § It's no small issue being in this world.

Finding the vault of heaven silent, it fills it with its chirp chirp.
Like Buddha it doesn't yearn for things that don't belong to it.
And again like Buddha it is silent. Contented.
Content because it wanted only to be a sparrow: and it is.
A sage. (Birds and sages are alike.)
Beautiful. Round-eyed. Merry.
And with light brown feathers.

It doesn't complain.
Admires nothing.
It's just like a horse. (Horses don't admire each other.)
Doesn't ask "Where am I?"
It's there.
A little silly, a little daft.
Of rabble nature. (Who isn't?)
But in truth, unhurried.[24]
A consummate humanist.[25]
As you'll see, with a half-monk, half-Brahmin soul.
It goes everywhere with hop hop tiny steps. (And why should it hurry?)
And like all of us, it believes in love and death.
And again like all of us, it learns by doing.
Thanks, sparrow.

---

24 Unhurried because it has no possibility of knowing what it has not lived.
25 It sits with me at the courtyard table (God thought up courtyards for birds). And
again it rises with me.

Dot / Dash

I

So here are two words with a lot to say:
Dot and Dash.
Dot was unloved right from the start.
Even Euclid doesn't want that word in his mouth.
'A thing without breadth' it says.
(But only breadth? It has no shadow. Let's say that too.)
There's nothing surprising in that.

A rationalist, a dictator, a commander.
But essentially an enemy of imagination: It starts off by wringing the neck of a beautiful word or sentence. Half way through it puts up barricades and makes a blockade of everything.
It finds the journey of creation tedious and wants to cut it short. And in this way does it squeeze the life from the act of writing, freeze it and leave it for dead.
But its insistence, its arrogance finds no entry into modern works: For page after page the shadow of a dot never falls.
Pythagoras would call the dot the First Being.
First and last.

II

There's no journeying with a dot.

The dot stays still as stone.

Knows no increase.

Arrogant, selfish.

Semiotics' most bigoted member: Hangs a sour face to the whole family, turns up its nose.

Regards the comma especially as an enemy: If it could, it would wipe it out entirely.

And yet who has the richness of a comma? It is, above all, a journeyman: There's nowhere it hasn't been.

It is ready to compete with time and space. What more could one ask?

The dot is an enemy of detail. It doesn't know that everything is in the details; it doesn't want to know. Maybe that's why it's angry with the comma.

Who know?

But of course no one loves the oppressor.

But that's how it is, eternity's vanguard (for some poets eternity is everything, while others turn their noses up at it!) It holds the hand of dash. And it's great.

And the dash does well in coming after dot, it finds its place wherever dot's shadow falls. Who wouldn't want that?

III

The dash is formed by a walking dot.

(Dots walk.) And the dash's nature is to gird on distance, like zero. Only distance? Future too. (Like eternity, the future has no beginning, no end.) No sooner was it created then it was shared. And so it isn't slow to take up its unique position in the history of things. On the other hand, it's the symbol of negativity: It carries its identity as a separator, a divider. When we compare it to dot (we can't compare it but) it's wrong in every respect. Unlike the dot, dash's being can't be tethered. It stretches out as fast as it can. It clears away anything in its path. (The history of speed should be documented.) It's self-propelling. It dons a variety of shapes but first it assumes the shape of an arch (dear arch) and sets off around the world, from one end to another. But not before calling in on Euclidian Geometry: It will step out with parallel and diagonal lines, with squares, climb with triangles, drop down into open-closed spaces. And in this way it tries out every possible shape before finally waking up to itself. As a dash, it's always on the go: as if it was looking for itself. (Doesn't everything have a past, a present, and a future, and one that it will live through?) And that's what it is to be a dash.

from **Long Live Numbers**

Like letters, numbers are individuals.

Their names are their shapes.
We cannot know or see their contents for their natures.
We can't see

      perhaps

          they

              choose

                    not to be seen,

(they retreat into their inner world) and peer out from there.

If they look at all.

And what is there to see, what will they see?
Isn't the world already too visible?
What's going to change if numbers expose themselves?
Shape is everything.
They've figured this out.
Anyway, no one cares about numbers.
Why should they?
Numbers are perfect.
(At any rate Mathematics is beautiful.)

What more could they want?

Only 1, is ambitious, dim.
Orders everything as it sees it.
Only it too is deprived of shape:

From up above

       to down

            below
            s
            t
            r
            e
            t
            c
            h
            i
            n
            g

it

    knows

        nothing

             else

Plato, only he, had a special love for **1**.
He never knows where to place it.
Should it surprise us, or not? I don't know.
Maybe he chose it because it's easy to write.
Or else it being vertical interested him.
Who doesn't like things vertical?
Really, how did Plato write **1**?
Perhaps it was enough for him to move his pen tip thus.

Yet if we look at Leonardo da Vinci's handwriting in the Vatican Palace
We see he felt no interest at all in **1**.

For him, **1** is something between existence and non-existence.

Pale, barely perceptible, as if he doesn't see it.
Did he look at it as if it lacked content?

PERHAPS.

1 is vast, especially 'vast' is one.
A book could even be written about **1**.
That may not even be enough.
Not enough, because **1**'s wound doesn't heal.
It's everything.
Above all it's a Theist.
(Who has escaped God?)
It's enough to know even this, isn't it?
But no, Plotinus takes the matter further.
For him, **1** is the son of God.
It's the world's right arm.
And like God it can't be grasped, comprehended with reason.
We can only say what **1** isn't, not what it is.
And not only that:
It's the foundation and pillar of the world.
And I can also say **1** blocks the way of poets.

(BECAUSE)

WHERE THERE

IS BEGINNING

THERE

IS

NO ETERNITY

While **1** pioneers its darkness
2, as if slashing with a knife, divides **1** in half.
1 is a Monist, **2** is a dualist.
And this they will always preserve.
Showing how **2** will rise against the absolute rule of **1**.
And this ought to be very welcome for innocent materialists.
Especially against **1** not counting it at all.

(OPPOSITES NEVER UNITE.)

2's hardheartedness comes, for sure, from **1** wanting to bind everything
        to itself.
Maybe secretly it's infuriated by **1**.
It wants, at least a little, to feel its strength.

Didn't

        the

                first

                        assault

on

        spirit

               come

                        from **2?**

Only **2** wasn't satisfied with this

   alone.   How ve

        ry

        mu

        ch

more it has to say

y

e

t

what could be greater than

c

o

n

t

r

a

d

i

c

t

i

o

n?

9

'IT WAS BEAUTIFUL WHEN THE CLOCK SHOWED NINE'

Dalí is very fond of **9**. He sees it as a faultless example of a cubic picture. **9** is actually esoteric. That's where its centre point is. To **10** (this twin nation neighbour) it claimed the world has no meaning. (**9** sees the world as a heap of shit.)

We've no idea what **10** had to say. But **9** knows that of all the paired numbers **10** is the most beautiful. But it may want to know if this beauty comes of it being the first of the paired numbers, or in being divisible (**10** is divisible like **2**) both in form and content. It might then conclude it views the world in darkness because it is a single number. (Because **9** sees itself as the loneliest of all numbers.) I wouldn't want to recommend loneliness to any number. Numbers are lonely enough as it is. And yet there is something humane in the loneliness of **9**. But I don't know if it's aware of it.

> *'Ten remained behind me, the ten before nine*
> *Not nine but ten*
> *Ten flowers, ten suns, ten Junes.'*

10 symbolizes perfection, wholeness.

10 has a huge world divided in two: Light, vast.
But when we say light, it's not everything, there's obscurity too. It can hardly be said the world has saved itself from openness, from obscurity. It's the incurable seed within us! Didn't things (the world we call silent) also take their share like all of us? The world we call silent calls out for parentheses: That's to say, nails, wheels, dusty roads, chairs, stones, windows, notebooks, pens, coal sacks; that's to say, whatever holds the poet's hand, all of that... And only poets? Do they not also tie the knot of reality?

Everything aside, **10** is the happiest number in the world. The thing we call life is **10**.

What about zer0?

All numbers live at rakish speed.
Especially zero.
The final demon!
The last discovery !

Hey,

Zero screams, saying *'I'm not a circle, I'm a zero.'* [26*]
It has a right, throughout heaven and earth. The source
is the source. And who would want that confused?

It didn't fall from a tree: like **1, 0**'s discovery—which required
only one step—has been a gigantic journey. While **1** is held
in great esteem, a leader, **0** is the last great discovery.
And because **0** never once lost hope in the future, the length
or brevity of the future never bothered it. Maybe that's why
it is the language of the future. And of this let no one be in
doubt: because the future is for all of us. And perhaps
it's only the future that cannot be taken away from anyone.
Again only the future can be given out and shared. This
isn't something to sniff at. It isn't satisfied only with the future.
It goes beyond it. Inscribes velocity.
Enormous speed:
It says 'Consider the velocity in multiplication, in growth!'

[26*] Plato didn't know zero. Neither did his disciple.

great

Whichever way we look at it, both in terms of shape and content, zero has no equal. As a shape, it's the shape of itself: it takes everything
within: it is everything. It never wavers. To give a name to everything, it is everything. An identifier. As contemporaneous as it is extant. Longevity is in its blood. We might say longevity is its self. With Al Harizmi's help, it reached all the way to now. How else could we explain it? An alien. Fearless!

marathon runner

Compared to **1** (zero is an earthling, it chose the world) it doesn't cling to God. Again unlike **1** it doesn't exile itself by climbing walls and ramparts trying to lay claim to everything. And **1** should understand that it's time has passed. It should leave God alone. It should recognize zero as the leader of a new age and retreat into the shade. Zero is the world's new Maestro!

The great chorus!
The language, of enlightenment!

symbol

And

which

number

of absence

assumes

     both

         endlessness

and

     abundance

  and

     finitude

I've read zero is a number that consumes all

These multi-digit numbers couldn't stop themselves meeting with the symbols in my private dictionary.

99 The **99** beautiful names of Allah.
100 'Let the Hundred Flowers Bloom.'
101 Atlas of Darkness (which is horribly sexual).
102 Pandora's box (that fears for its life at night).
103 Postman of the East (the poem's long horizon).
108 Titivilus (that classic under the pillow).
120 The Angel of Death (the seventh stratum of suffering).
144 St. John's dear number (adorning the skirts of Mount Zion).
153 Is loneliness, History.
216 Is the Golden Oriole with three souls.
300 The great leveller (is the sick-house of **300** blind).
432 Station of Transitions (is surrounded by hanging gardens).
440 The Hell Readier.
441 Maria Magdelena (the revue girl, a child-woman).
1000 The Auditor of Death.
1001 Wounded Eros.

Take the numbers from everything, they will all rot.
Isidoré

Nothing escapes form. Because form is everything. Numbers are the same. Is being such as small thing? What more could be wanted? Painters are the first to recognize numbers for their shapes. And the first of them was Magritte.

Magritte loves playing with numbers. He had a casual interest in mathematics. Everyone has a way of doing things (in their own fashion).

But only him? What about the guy who painted them

Pop artist

Jasper   Johns

who   painted

portraits   of **1** to **9**

but   somehow

left   **0**   out

neither   its form

nor   content

interested   him

considering it   perhaps

midway   between

existence   and

absence

And 'absence' is an act much like zero. Emptiness
is fullness too. We shouldn't be afraid but just
go along with it. Jaspers ought to know this too.
O should be put in its place. Above all
we ought to extract the magic of zero.
Because zero *is* magical: it spreads magic.
Any time, any place there it is before us.
And who can do without it?
Perhaps he never saw **O**, and knows nothing
of it. Why not? Besides, zero isn't a
number, it's numberlessness.
But from painters we learn to look
at numbers as though they were pictures.
Otherwise we'd just say numbers are numbers.
For example: before Franz Kline
the number **8** was no different
from any other number. Through him
we saw **8**'s enchanting beauty.
And we hung it on our walls like that.
Numbers haven't escaped the painter's
hand. So the abstract world of numbers
became ever more our world.
But still something is always missing:
Their voices! ('Their voices
are the semblance of being')
No one has wanted to know their voice.

It's still the same.

Numbers are a forest of symbols:

1/ Is faceless.
    (Second-hand birds, insects, children)
2/ Innocent moralist.
    (Long hair, long nights and unwound silk)
3/ Virgin Mary.
    (Blood, Aztecs, forests, water's memory)
4/ Other worldly.
    (The repressed, shoved aside, flat-footed)
5/ Passionate love.
    (Djinns, elephants, gold inspectors)
6/ Distant shore (melancholy)
    (Netters, diviners of water, bees)
7/ Colour blind.
    (Undreaming, days wondering around)
8/ Monist.
    (Hairpins, yellow buttons, white scissors)
9/ Reticent love.
    (Idle rivers, those living near their banks, misty mornings)
0/ Auto "I" (sorrowful)
    (Ants, aquatic flies, goat tracks)

We would never know numbers, if they weren't such exposed entities. Their lives, their identities are indebted to counting. Suppose we never hold their hands, it's as if their very existence were thrown into doubt, they don't reveal themselves and turn around and around in the same place.

> Numbers live inside everything, and outside too.
> They assume a shape, but do not move from one to another.
> (Everything has a dilemma; theirs is this.)
> Some intellectuals have been fascinated by numbers.
> Chief among them, Aristotle.

Secretly he likes **1**, but he only touches it lightly and doesn't take it on (**1** has seven souls, like the number **7** too, so let's forgive it here). Perhaps it doesn't want to be overly familiar with God (God forces us to talk about him, and he loves it). And we can't prove **1** with reason, nor refute it. (**1** says it comes from the same race as Thales; and like Thales, it sleeps with water, wakes with water.)

And this is also a truth: that we cannot set out without **1**, for if ever we do, we stumble. And in repeating **1** we find **2**, which is everything. Everything, because it opens the way before us. We are indebted to it for our intimacy with life today.[27*] And we can't think without numbers, we can't even do the simplest thing. (Here is the perfect place to make the thinker's ears ring, for without them we couldn't even approach numbers. Foremost, without Kant. These days they spare precious little time for numbers. Dear Hartmann [they say his bed is in his paternal house] is interested only in the living—only them—and knows nothing else. Kierkegaard, Husserl and Heidegger opened parentheses only for "being". Perhaps they wanted me to come and explain it all, so the pleasure I take in it is my right.)

[27*] **2**, sees itself as a tree-lined street.

from House

Door

A voice: how many handprints on the door?

How to form the equation
to find the door?
Add, subtract,
or divide?

$$\begin{array}{r} \text{House} \\ \text{Window} \\ \text{x} \\ \hline \text{Door}^{28^*} \end{array}$$

In the world there is no sovereignty above that
of the door's.
House, is a door.

First door, then house.

It knew this, right from the start. All precautions were taken for this (it
being a door).

No matter how, if the house limits its name and its presence, be it limits
without doors, there can be no house.

There is no house without the door.
Everything comes and goes by way of the door.
The door serves none but itself.

Indeed, the door is a commander, a power-monger like the wall; we
        should accept it for this too.

28* 'Doors, open to empty living rooms.'

Everything is asked of me, says the door's heart.

See, a woman has come along and stopped, reached out too for the knocker, was about to reach out her hand.

She sees it for the first time.
What else is she going to do but knit her brows?

Door = house

Has it become a house?

There is no house

The house is to die in.

Room

The nature of the house is silence.
Rooms, sofas, stairs, furniture weave silence.

THE HOUSE DEMANDS SILENCE.

House is a winding ball of narrow paths. These narrow paths feed it.
It scatters such silence, limitlessness.
Lives everything fully in this quietude.
(This is the single thing that's shared in the house.)

House is the room.

An island.
(In its own state)
a call within.
In praise of confinement, loneliness.
But we always see a house.
The house is in fact the spectator.
Wanders around, as if it's not there.
Opens, closes doors.
In the house everything is there for each other.
(Confinement requires it.)
Only the room lives for itself.
The house has a dream for every situation.
The room is forever watchful.
The room talks about everything.
There's a meaning to everything too.
(Nothing can escape meaning.)

Man is an island.

The room: A world.

Window

$$\frac{\text{House}\quad\text{Leaf}\quad —}{\text{Window}}$$

Foresees the solution to every equation.
So then: THE WINDOW
An eye (seeing all inside the brackets).
Partitioning, encoding, freezing still.
An image predator.
Where in the house, it says, is better to see outside?
(Window believes the view is there for itself.)
Its presence too is indebted to absence.
It has grabbed the world before it.
(The window faces forward.)

Is it a child passing by?

'A child's passing!' it will say.

Is it ice cream a woman is coming to eat?

'A woman is coming to eat ice cream'
it will say.

Is it the sun rising?

— Thanks sun! it will say.

But this too will not suffice, it will announce what it sees to the interior;
        (in any case the interior wants this).

Such is the window, since everything is there for the inside.
— Who's that beating the glass?
— A straying cloud.
— A leaf.

The window is everything.

Wall I

'Mother, must the walls be so high?'

House is something of a wall.

We could say it's something that doesn't move.
But it doesn't stay just by staying still.
It divides, cuts off, closes (closing is its job).
But we don't see, we don't know the wall.
The house is doors, balconies, windows, stairs.
It's the plumbing too.
The wall hides.
Masquerades as a thinker.
Doesn't give itself up.

If we happen upon a wall, it's a door we compare it too.
It too hides itself like a wall.

Wall considers door of its own kind.
A prohibitor, an authority like itself.
Perhaps this is why from the very beginning it never adopted openness.
Sincere, loquacious too like a window.[29*]

_____

29* For sure, we shouldn't expect the wall to understand the door. I don't.

In the history of being
(the history of being is a history of imperceptibles) it's as if the wall
          alone has no meaning.
Right away it reminds us of the house.[30*]

Without the house, its being is doubtful.

We should embrace it for this.
Such a presence.

Those in the house
Beware of walls!

30* I ask you, wall, how is it you're indestructible?

Wall II

By its nature, the wall interrogates everything.
— What's behind the wall?
If it's this garden wall, then the garden; if the house, then the house, it
      cross-examines the house's interior.
So it is, the wall builds its metaphor of secrecy from the beginning.
What's curious too, it does this by driving its curiosity bugs back and
forth.
Every wall shoulders this.
And slowly secrecy becomes the walls reason to exist.
For sure, the wall is not aware of this.
It knows nothing of this.
Besides, wall is a house.
It's a house, thus it justifies itself.
Later, it's in the house we more often come across the wall.
But to say that is no more than a hypothesis.
Because we don't see the wall at home.
If we put it like Jacques Peret, we only see the wall when we hang
      something on it.
And for sure when we bang our heads against it.
And just for a while.
Then we immediately forget.
The wall is secrecy.
Secrecy, the wall's incurable destiny.
It cannot be escaped.

Wall III

Everywhere we're as close to walls as flesh to bones.
When the window, door, balcony, ceiling etc. are a part of the house,
the
              wall is everything.
We wander in the house from wall to wall.
But the wallets no one sense its dominance.
It never opens up without thinking first.
For sure, this too is its virtue.
As with all things, the phenomenon of walls (why don't we say its
              poetics?) is silence.
It is wounded with silence.
This too it scatters through the house.
A great, enchanted silence.
Open to everything.
The wall grants us this.

The wall is open reading.
Miracle-filled.
(Where aren't there miracles?)
It's enough to read it.
Walls render us speechless.
There's no escaping walls.

Wall IV

Wall is a discovery.
When the house (the house's logos) induces dreams of richness, it's as if
       the wall excludes itself. It distances itself from everything.
It doesn't share the house.
It behaves as if there were no house.
Only the house?
It doesn't count itself among the towns, the squares, the gardens it encloses
       and surrounds.
It lives by withdrawing from everything.
It has chosen aloneness.
As windows, doors, balconies, rooms, ceilings and cupboards live together,
       wall is like the stranger of the house.
It's Penelope.
Nose to the ground.
Doesn't complain, doesn't beg.
In order not to reveal itself it hides its appearance; throws away, cleans out
       all of its corners and outer edges.
Its power too (the dominance of a wall) it reduces to zero.
It can't be said this is what the wall wants.
Who wants loneliness?
Still, it must mean something to the wall.
But we'll never learn this.

Everywhere the wall is alone.
The wall doesn't smile.

Summation

I love all stone walls, especially those at the entrance to roads, I love huge, old, neglected, abandoned stone walls between a shabby, ruined fence. I hear their voices. A vanished, magical world stirs within stones: it calls us to mysterious travels. Stones have no egos, or else there is an I that's wandering. Stones are always stones. (Nothing is complex, unless man complicates it.) I once wrote that I wanted to be a stone mason, a wall builder. Wall masons are happy people. They can see the work they do: they touch, hold with the hand. In Halicarnassos there are wall masons, and walls, I've made friends with. Many of them are stored in my memory. I can't pass one of them without saying hello. I've witnessed walls talk. I've heard their vast silence. Lived through their epic poem. I've run my hand around and over them all. I've idolized them all.

It's still the same.

A Turtledove Valantin Taskin

Valantin Taskin was born in a stately home in Caucasia in 1902.

He played with dolls to the age of three and with his beloved father's beard.

By the age of six he knew every bird by sound and name.

At seven he started piano lessons. The world was his.

At ten he played Chopin in front of the Char family.

He learned languages. "However many languages there are, that's how many worlds there are" his father had said. He never forgot it.

At seventeen picture books, maps of the world were forever in his hands.

He always likened himself to Sleeping Beauty.

At eighteen he married Constantin Clodt von Jürgenzburg. He separated one year later.

At twenty he developed a passion for insects. He found beauty in all that insects did.

He started a stamp collection. He believed he had come into the world in the form of a turtledove.

A diamond brooch and a pair of golden earrings were all he saved from the revolution. He cried his heart out in Istanbul.

Then suddenly he remembered he could play the piano. He accompanied the orchestra of La Bohème at the Lüx Hayat hotel.

He played the mazurka in Tavernas. And met Todori.

For forty years now Todori sings while he plays.

Now in every photograph he's staring off into the distance, suddenly jolted by the way he's lived his life.

Denizens of Hristaki Arcade

I don't love evenings anymore, said Diran, there was a time when I loved evenings so much.

I don't want to remember anything. Why remember?

Everything's changed and left its place to a huge silence.

Mari still hasn't come back, said Ifijeni. Paluka must have shut up shop ages ago.

Why is it this Alba's breasts are so big, said Vartuhi, she's not even fourteen.

She's like her mother, said Marta, there was a time her breasts had no equal in Pera.

How many times did I tell you to have Izidor cut your hair, said Armenak, it's driving me mad.

Everything of yours gets on my nerves, everything.

How crowded Papillon's tat shop is, said Glavani, it's impossible to understand these women.

Memories make me fat like this, said Diran, from now on I don't want to touch another thing.

It's enough for me to look out of the window. See, Eleni is coming back, a blue bag in her hand.

She always wears high heeled shoes, always goes out alone.

Pigmalion has changed its display again, said Sara, stores don't know what to do.

What's your problem, said Marta, all day you jabber on like that.

So what? Don't you hear them every night making love upstairs, that's what I'm on about, said Sara.

Then they drink Chinese tea till evening and sit staring at the sky, I just don't get it.

The sky is ribbons, rag dolls, picture books, oranges from China.

This Luisa is now in her sixties, said Diran, and she still can't tear her head from the window.

Every night Lebon, Alkazar, Degustasion! She never gets enough of the world.

Every night, every night it's Hafiz Burhan, Osman Nihat, Hafiz Cemaon the old 78s.

Lulu's become very forgetful, said Germaine, she keeps asking how much water to put with the rice.

Yesterday she left the house to go to Shűtte and found herself in Saint Terre church.

We've grown old, old, I can't even pick up two logs of wood from here to throw on the stove.

How many times have I told Yanni to bring me dry wood, he doesn't understand.

My side's been burning for a while, I'm shaking, said Eleni, and the doctor says I've nothing.

But I should sleep early, get up early, avoid getting cold, look after my health.

I also said that some mornings I wake up as a butterfly; these things happen.

So Sara has closed her windows, said Marta, she could never stop thinking about her husband who went away to sea on a banana boat.

Look how long Miss Suzan's neck is, Said Lulu, who does she look like?

There was a time when she couldn't care less, she wore yellow socks and bedded whoever she pleased.

Ulla is shouting again from the third floor that she's going to Markiz, said Diran.

Is she going to Markiz, said Madam Tilla, I hate the smell of resin, never liked it.

I saw Doctor Violi yesterday, said Eleni, when I was coming back from the Royal Hotel; he didn't recognize me.

He used to wave to me from Marta's window; how I used to laugh.

His house smelt always of carnations and oil; I came and went through the smell of carnations and oil.

For months, said Armenak, I've no desire to go to Nektar, right under my nose; what happened to me?

Beyoğlu is like a shroud now, no, a vinegar!

See, it's night, said Diran, we should close the windows, night has come.

Night, now, everything is night, for one or two hundred years, everything is night.

The world is full of loneliness, said Lulu, one minute I'm watering geraniums, the next I'm changing my clothes.

Ah, it never ends, said Armenak, that damned noise from downstairs, these sounds of drums and flutes.

I can't sleep looking at Margarita's hat and umbrella, said Marko.

How beautifully she used to sing those Tuscany ballads sitting right in front of me.

Now Time doesn't know how to pass: children, trees, the water-dead in water.

The smell of Matilda's skin, said Vartuhi, more than anything I can't forget that smell.

Her silk stockings, and her long legs, and her sleeping all night with a rose in her mouth.

And now at four o'clock I'm tossing and turning in my bed, tossing and turning.

This world's strangling me, this house, this window, these curtains, this toothbrush.

This is Madam Anahit's accordion, said Matilda, I grew up with this accordion.

Now she's playing those beautiful comparsitas and tangos to this dirty crowd.

Ah, I can't listen anymore to her butcher's songs, her onion smelling accordion.

This city, these walls, these radio noises are driving me crazy.

You're so right, said Suzan, I don't want to see this Long Road, these trees, these people anymore.

ALL TOGETHER

Forgive us, forgive us all you houses, streets, people, forgive us.

Forgive us old age, forgive us.

Nevizade Street Greengrocer Ahmet Aslanoğlu

Thirty-five years Ahmet Aslanoğlu opened and closed Nevizade Street.
He loved green and knew no other colour but green.

For a long part of his childhood he observed the flight of birds.
He didn't understand birds at all.

In his old age (has it come to that already?)
The wine's bitter taste changed nothing.

When his work went well—for whatever reason—
He believed that God had suddenly sat on the sky.

Evenings he saw Orhan and Sait leaving Lambo
As they passed he always raised a smile behind their backs.

For thirty-five years Ahmet Aslanoğlu was a greengrocer
For thirty-five years he painted Nevizade Street green.

Madrigals

I Came to You Always with a Piece of Sky

1. Look for me there in the rivers at night, there in the rivers at night.

2. I came to you always with a piece of sky.

3. I came in the attire of olden times and with a black moustache.

4. I set myself up there as the balcony of an old house.

5. I used to stop and wave my fist to the trees and never leave.

6. Love is a shadow.

Small Villages Birds Cats Dogs

1. I saw the water run slow in Egypt.

2. Legend has it, one day the water-fly will set off with the silkworm.

3. Small villages birds cats dogs.

4. And the face of women…

5. We lived beneath such grey skies grey histories.

6. In those days I was a blonde haired kid, I used to say let them think that way about me.

It's True I Sometimes Turn to Rivers and Trees

1. Ithaca is always the same.

2. A forest a house prepares for night.

3. A tree steps forward it wants to say something.

4. It's true I sometimes turn to rivers and trees.

5. Who hasn't had that?

A River Moves Around Like a Peasant

1. I saw time I saw the emptiness I saw their youth.

2. I saw that time was grey, everything grey, grey.

3. A river moves around like a peasant.

4. I saw and now I'm telling you eternity is everywhere.

5. You undressed me like this as if watering a flower.

6. We get better as we kiss.

It Was Then the Self-Explaining World Came and Started Its Work

1. For you I'm planting trees collecting stones for you.

2. Pirates Vikings Andalusian Arabs and thunder for you.

3. And salt.

4. You would come your magic mouth embroidering dead butterflies on my eyelids.

5. And smoke.

6. It was then the self-explaining world came and started work.

That Was You Thin As a Leaf

1. History is loneliness and we used to embrace tightly and lie down.

2. That was you thin as a leaf.

3. At night your eyes are magical your mouth you would drop your hair and leave.

4. You would say sea-swallows fly close to the ground.

5. You were like a naked willow branch.

6. I was dry moss and an animal fresh out of its cave.

It Should Be Evening Where You Are Now

1. You were flames flashes and endless time.

2. We were those stones irons and blind wells.

3. We used to smell mouldy sheets and childhood scents.

4. Everything changes when you look close.

5. It should be evening where you are now.

6. I used to call you 'half of the sky' and I just wouldn't stop talking.

We Used to Use a Water Clock & a Sundial

1. We used to use a water clock & a sundial.

2. We were swarthy skinny like beetle-browed books.

3. We were low hunters who gathered food and hunted a little.

4. In bad weather we woke with the grey smell of loneliness.

5. They were upper hunters catching fish and placing them in clean salty water.

6. We were more like silence we looked out from there.

As If We Were Like Blacked Out Days

1. The word has no time and life is dark.

2. We were alone we'd follow three steps behind you and everything was water.

3. The camels were peevish the horses used to whinny.

4. You passed through with bell-flowers ants and snapdragons in your mouth.

5. As if we were like blacked out days.

6. Like a crumpled tissue I just wouldn't straighten out.

Ask Night About Me in Time and Space

1. We were talking about these passing clouds.

2. You say stone and wind have no future.

3. You know love turns to itself too.

4. I who wrote eternity always eternity.

5. Ask night about me in time and space.

6. Taint me with your silver mouth my iris.

www.ingramcontent.com/pod-product-compliance
Lightning Source LLC
Chambersburg PA
CBHW030545030726
47495CB00004B/1145